WORDS LIKE
FIRE
WORDS THAT GET RESULTS

KENT B. SMITH

BALBOA.
PRESS
A DIVISION OF HAY HOUSE

Balboa Press books may be ordered through booksellers or by contacting:

Balboa Press
A Division of Hay House
1663 Liberty Drive
Bloomington, IN 47403
www.balboapress.com
1 (877) 407-4847

Print information available on the last page.

ISBN: 978-1-9822-0958-2 (sc)
ISBN: 978-1-9822-0959-9 (e)

Balboa Press rev. date: 11/13/2018

ACKNOWLEDGMENTS

The road to writing this book has been full adversities, pitfalls and barriers, but my family has always believed I would one day complete the journey. April, Briana, Chris and Demetrius all of your emotional support is greatly appreciated. I know my typed words can only begin to express how much your belief in me meant. During the times of adversity, your love helped me to stay the course. "Thank You" for the days our shared moments had to be brief; the movie nights I had to forego; and for all the times I rehearsed the information I'd learned by giving you advice (even when not requested).

The author of countless spoken books...Mrs. Omentha L. Smith-Crowe (mom) has imparted in me the desire, wisdom and the tenacity to reach beyond my circumstances. You are my mother and my friend. You shaped my life with the power of understanding. God had given me a bright future because he placed you in charge of loving me through the times I couldn't see what I could be and praying until God's vision for me became clear. I love, appreciate and respect you.

There has never been one moment that my Pastor and friend G.E. Studdard, Jr., never doubted that I would be able to complete the task of sharing wisdom through this book. I appreciate every word of encouragement you spoke to or concerning me. You are proof that words have power. The insight you have given me into "How the WORD is processed; information, meditation, revelation, application, and demonstration" is one of the key elements that ignited the desire to write this book.

"Unwavering dedication to a specific goal will bring success if that goal is flexible, obtainable, meditated on and consistently acted on." (Studdard Jr. 2005).

In loving memory: Camila and Wix Smith laid the foundation and planted the seeds that would later place me in front of dignitaries from all around the world. They never let me forget, "wisdom is the principal thing, so get wisdom and with all your getting, get understanding" (Proverbs 4:7). Chastised and corrected, but always mentored and deeply loved. That is how they guided my life even after they were gone.

DEDICATION

Special Mention: My close friend whom I never met.

One Sunday I was in a church service, I felt my phone vibrate. I usually would ignore it but something made me look at the text. The Battalion Sergeant Major asked me to assist another unit by performing Casualty Assistance duty. That means I had to go help the family of a fallen soldier. Nineteen-year-old Specialist Branigan Bahney died in an automobile accident. I had been trained for this kind of assignment, but this would be my first time doing it. Later that evening I received the rest of the information to contact the family. I had to call a grieving mother to express the condolences of the U.S. Government and offer my help. There are no simple words which can ease the pain of losing someone you love.

Part of my dilemma was I had just learned to manage my emotions after my deployment the year prior. While I was away on deployment, my younger stepbrother passed away. A few months after I returned home, my wife and I separated after 25 years. But the hardest part was SPC Bahney was the same age as my daughter.

SPC Bahney's mother set the tone for the conversation. She told me where the arrangements were being made and I agreed to meet her there. The family and I met at the funeral home which was about a two hour drive from my home. The first task was to make sure they knew my heart went out to them and I was really there to serve. I sat and tried not to interfere with the conversations. There were several times I reassured SPC Bahney's mother that I was there to help with anything she deemed the family needed. Hearing myself say those words I thought, "How could they know that I really mean it?" My prayer was that she would grow to understand that serving her and the family was an honor, not just my job.

All the family members were open and honest. They seemed to be united in love for each other and for SPC Branigan. They even made me feel welcomed as if I were a part of the family throughout the whole arrangement process.

As I began to assist them with various items, I would hear different stories about this young soldier "Branigan Bahney". Bran, as they called him, was kind to everyone. He always had a smile on his face. He loved to make people laugh. He befriended the people others pushed away. He would dance and sing pretty much anywhere, just to have a good time and make sure that others did as well. He was a man of faith in God. He was honest, hardworking, fun loving and thoughtful. Anyone he met became a friend.

The sincerity of God's love showing through him was evident by the steady flow of people, both young and old, who for 5 hours came to wish him farewell. I became kind of envious of Branigan. Although he was only 19 years old, he allowed the power of a good heart to make him into the man I am still struggling to be. I didn't know him during his life, but he still became one of my closest friends. The power of Bran's communication wasn't only in the words he spoke, it was in his life magnificently well lived.

"Let my words be like fire and the people's heart as wood, that every word I speak ignites a fire within them." Kent B. Smith

CONTENTS

FOREWORD

Wisdom is the principal thing, so get wisdom. And with all your getting get understanding. (Proverbs 4:7, NKJ)

Inspire

My burning question is…What's that element that makes speakers effective? The factor that actually reaches people and motivates them to do something. For example, it might be the passion in a singer's voice that stirs and moves one's soul or the emotions that actors exhibit in a play that an audience can relate to. These expressions and attributes relay passion, emotion, commitment, and desire. They make your mind, will and emotions tingle. These words set your soul ablaze in anticipation of some pending exciting experience or the re-experience of a previous emotional state.

Webster, Oxford and Macmillan dictionaries' have a general consensus of definition of the term inspire as meaning to stir, arouse, move, encourage or motivate. It comes from inspiration, in Latin, this term means to breathe or the breath. When someone speaks words that ignite your soul, they are saying "take a breather…a moment to get motivated; to be encouraged; to get stirred up by the gifts lying dormant inside you; to arouse the power of your self-worth, and be moved to action."

There are many forms of motivation and even hundreds of more people using those various forms of motivation, but does the instant thrill have a lasting effect? Can the one being motivated reproduce the motivation without an outside source? The difference between inspiration and motivation is motivation gives the reason(s) one has for acting or behaving in a particular way. Inspiration is the process of being mentally energized or stimulated to the point of action or feel something, especially, to do something creative. Also, inspiration is the drawing in of breath; inhalation; to draw in life force (Merriam-Webster).

The term "like fire" means "the attribute of having dynamic energizing influence on people and things; the catalyst for change." Fire is a powerful elemental force that can be unpredictable, if unrestrained, just like words. But also like words, fire can bring energy, light and life when used properly. One of the attributes of fire is that it follows the path which it can consume, not always the path of least resistance. It will consume everything in its path. Fire is like a living organism; it will go toward what it can feed on and make that item a part of the fire. When fire meets an object it can't easily consume, it will eventually transform that item, as long as the intensity of the fire can be increased.

Words are meant to ignite the imagination. The imagination is the beginning of all things under heaven. God formed what He wanted in His mind, then He spoke it into existence. Our words work in much the same manner but are imperfect. We imagine imperfectly. We speak with imperfect faith. That's why we have to imagine and speak in repetition. During the repetition, we begin to imagine more clearly and believe more deeply. Our words take on the authority of faith, which causes our action to line up with our beliefs.

Words like Fire are life altering statements. Hollywood has dramatized power phrases to make it seem as though a Jedi mind trick is being performed. The real power of words is not a trick; it's finding the point of influence. In other words, it is understanding which words or phrases reach the core thoughts and emotions of the intended person. Words which cause change carry many of the same attributes of the elemental object, fire.

It seems like fire has been written about by millions of authors. Many writers mentioning fire relate its power to that of God. One such writing in recent times stated, "It may be surprising to many Christians that the word "fire" and its attributes of "light" and "heat" speak more of the Creator and His goodness than of a destructive force against His enemies" (Tentmaker Ministries, n.d., para 2).

The Creator Himself is described as an "All Consuming Fire" (Deut. 4:24; Heb. 12:29). The author (Tentmaker Ministries, n.d.) continues to say "Doesn't it seem rather strange to our understanding to call the Creator a consuming fire? Rarely, if ever, do we associate fire with the creation process. We usually associate it with destruction" (para. 9).

Fire has played perhaps one of the most significant roles in the advancement of civilization. My belief is that apart from the use of fire to break down and shape material for our use, manufacturing would be impossible. Our very lives depend upon the energy given by the biggest fire near the earth, the sun. Well, technically the sun's heat and energy produced by fusion. It's not a ball of fire, but it sure makes a great metaphor and the attributes are amazingly similar.

Many Christian believers understand that once they have allowed the fire of God to enter every area of their lives, they will see His fire in a totally different light. Rather than being utterly destroyed by the fire, they believe we are purified, corrected, cleansed. The fire of God within brings forth love which creates an environment of healing and restoration to all mankind. Spiritually minded people who desire to be changed, and who are willing to be conformed to the image of Christ do not fear the fire in the Bible.

They are more likely to use the word fire in a positive sense. I believe they are also more likely to be spiritually alive.

When we take a more detailed look at the attributes of fire, we find the ambient radiation and the light given off by fire are only the forerunners to the power of fire. Through modern science, we have learned various methods and equations for releasing the fire from within such as heat used to turn iron ore and carbon into steel; and the controlled combustion in an automobile engine. We call this conversion.

Fire is not constrained to science and industry alone. The arts and literature use fire as a metaphor. How many songs written about being encouraged, staying strong, strengthening yourself and being confident use fire as a point of reference? These are terms associated with the inner force of strength, the capacity to endure, the ability to overcome, and the passion to the point of accomplishment; or an inner fire. Bringing the force of fire from objects is a major feat to behold, but understanding how to use the fire in us is one of the most powerful lessons we could ever learn.

Meditate

My pastor said, "When you meditate on something long enough it becomes your reality." This means it becomes real to you. Not only that, but once you become more certain in your thought process, your words become more powerful. When the doubt is gone, your words take on authority as you speak to others. You cause actions to happen. Remember words are containers. If you fill that container with power and authority, when it's opened, power and authority come out. Teach yourself how to paint pictures with your mind. Learn how to build a mental foundation in your mind. One means of doing that is by envisioning yourself accomplishing the task that stands in front of you.

A person's reality is not made up of outside influences. One's reality actually consists of their thoughts, beliefs and mindset. This is the reoccurring theme that will shape your life. As a man (or woman) continues to think and meditate, life will begin to conform to that inner vision (good or bad). If we learn how to help people shape a specific thought process, then we can help them change their lives.

If your words are filled with intimidation and fear, they will contain just that...they will be weak...they won't have the burning resilience to overtake and change negative situations in your life.

This is why we teach the process of words in relation to thought as information, meditation, revelation, application and demonstration. (Studdard) When words are meditated on, those words will become a strong force within you. That word will become powerful. Emotions play a big part in your meditation. Are you painting your picture with a muddy boot or are you using a fine tip brush to bring out magnificent details? You can build the foundation of your thoughts with fragile bricks made of chalk, which are ready to crumble or from bricks tempered by a fire that are strong enough to withstand harsh weather.

Excitement

Fire needs a catalyst, fuel, and ignition. The fire we use in relation to people is the excitement we build which motivates the mind to the point of energizing the body for action. There are many different catalysts such as emotion, smell, sounds and familiarity to name a few. In science, the term excitement is used in describing the relationship of particles in a moving energetic state. The power of the atom comes from the amount of potential movement or excitement of the particles in it.

Atoms do not always remain in their ground state. An atom is said to be in an "excited state" when an electron occupies an orbital at a greater than normal distance from its nucleus. An atom in such an excited state has a greater than normal amount of energy. An atom can become excited in one of two ways: the atom can absorb energy by colliding with one or more particles such as another atom or from a source of electromagnetic radiation. Scientists have found that though an atom can be energized to a much higher excited state, the electron cannot stay in a higher orbital forever; the ground state is the only level where it can remain indefinitely.

In terms of the human excited state, powerful speakers may be able to instill in a person or group of people an energetic mindset. Like with an atom, a good motivational speaker can get multiplied excitement when they involve other excited people in the process. The listeners may be rallied together and become eager to take action, but it is in the calm ground state that direction and purpose for the excited action will shape into the long-term results.

One of my greatest friends and mentor, G.E. Studdard Jr., a pastor and motivational speaker taught, "Preaching will stir the soul and excite you to take action; teaching will settle you into a specific course of action" (June 2003). His instruction explains that on any given Sunday there will be people gathered together at any given church. Those people will hear a sermon full of thrilling and exciting words. They will clap, leap, and dance expressing great joy in the emotions of the meeting. Those same people will leave and declare, "Wow! Church service was great! We sure had a great service today." But when asked, "What did he preach about?" The reply would be, "I don't remember, but it sure was good."

This may sound funny, but in many cases it's true. Week after week people go to get stirred up, but little change happens to improve the character or standard of living for the listener. The same is true when corporations and organizations invite powerful speakers to motivate and inspire people to be energized to greater productivity. The information shared is right on point, but the excitement is difficult to maintain. However, the same information can be shared in a way that both teaches and reaches.

What's the element that makes inspirational speakers effective? Can you pinpoint what actually reaches people and motivates them to do something? Is it the passion in a singer's voice that stirs and moves the soul? Or, are the actions written into a play that causes the audience to feel every emotion the actors present? These expressions and attributes relay passion, emotion, commitment, and desire.

These words set your soul ablaze. Speakers make your mind, will and emotions tingle with anticipation about something better to come. "It is the supreme art of the teacher to awaken joy in creative expression and knowledge." Albert Einstein

Intro to Fire

Words being like fire means that we can communicate with intensity and relay POWER through various means of communication.

From the dawn of the first man feeling the burning heat of the sun beaming down on him, mankind has embraced fire as a source of great power. Many of the ancient cultures had deemed fire as an elemental force which was thought of as both creative and destructive. Unlike other elemental forces, fire is a power which lays dormant on the inside of all other elements.

Although fire meets some of the criteria for the scientific definition of life because it moves, breathes, consumes, and reproduces, I am not suggesting that fire is really a living being. Neither is this a suggestion of anything weird like projecting of human characteristics on to an inanimate object, such as fire. What I am suggesting is that our communication has similar attributes as fire. The characteristics and attributes of fire are simply metaphoric similitudes of the behavior between fire in comparison to human conduct and speech.

Fire refuses to stay small, just as a child has the need to grow. Like a teenager hitting a growth spurt, a fire will consume everything around it and will seem to have a contrary attitude toward anything that tries to add structure to its existence. Fire mandates independence and change as if it were in a fight to stay alive. It has some predictable traits, such as the rate of combustion, yet, fire can act in an unpredictable manner.

Fire, as the Force of Illumination

Light is a form of radiant energy which makes it possible for us to see the world around us. In philosophy, religion and in education the term light or illumination means to make something to be viewed clearly or to gain a greater understanding, this is where the phrase "to shed light on the subject" was derived and also, the term enlightened.

It is rumored ancient Buddhists taught that the meditation of observing and focusing on the beauty of life in all living things would bring enlightenment. In doing this, the Buddhist monks are said to have learned to focus intensely and mastered their own bodies to the point of doing superhuman feats. G.E. Studdard taught that broken focus is one of the most prevalent reasons why people don't accomplish things or obtain what they search after (2015).

Religious leaders have long told their followers to shape the world around them, by first changing how they think. "As a man thinketh in his heart, so is he" (Proverbs 23:7 KJV). This powerful statement has come to us in various forms: "You are and can have whatever you believe you can have or be"; "one's life is made up from the things he thinks he can achieve." The phrase "as a man thinketh" means when a person continues to think about and meditate on something. The phrase "so is he" refers to the act of meditating on a subject until it is ingrained in his subconscious so intensely that it will cause him to call on all of his internal and external resources to bring him the ability to possess the object of his meditation.

Simply put, as you think your thoughts become your subconscious beliefs. Your beliefs act like a Lego set. One belief builds on another. They become tightly fitted together. That "belief set" will then drive your emotions, decisions and actions, which will shape your world.

Many educators, philosophers, psychologists and motivators have tried to communicate this concept, in simplistic ways to make it easy to achieve. Even the street thugs believe things like, "If you act like a baller long enough, you'll be one", at least in your own eyes.

Some amazing information came from a comparison of the human mind to the most sophisticated man-made device ever created, the computer. The average computer can hold about 250,000 to 500,000 pictures; well over 21,000 songs and thousands of videos. We can store these items on a device that is no bigger than your thumb. Now let's compare it to your mind. Your mind can perform a rough estimate based on the number of digital electrical pulses (action potentials) that the approximately 100,000,000,000 or 10^{11} neurons in a human brain send to one another per second via approximately 10^{14} contacts (synapses) suggests that an adult human brain carries out about one thousand trillion (10^{15}) logical operations per second operations per second without you even consciously knowing it (http://www.phy.duke.edu/~hsg/363/table-images/brainvs- computer.html).

Ask yourself right now, "What's making my blood flow through your veins with the perfect amount of pressure to keep me alive? What's making your heart beat right now? Are you consciously telling your heart to beat? What's maintaining your body core temperature to the perfect degree to keep you alive? An even better question is, what's doing the greater than 6 trillion things to your over 50 trillion cells every single second of your life. It's your autonomic nervous system in conjunction with the subconscious mind. This is the dynamo at the center of who you are and what you can do.

Even with all of the mind's great ability, it has a simple but overwhelming limitation. The mind can hardly distinguish the difference between a real event and something you merely think about. Two examples are dreams and placebos.

Think about what happens when you have a nightmare. Your heart beats faster. Your breathing increases in depth and speed; sometimes you sweat heavily; you may even cry or yell. Your body didn't understand that you weren't in any real danger. Your body was reacting to what was playing out in your mind. Your body physiologically reacted to what was taking place only in your mind.

Placebos are used in the medical application of a perceived treatment to get a tangible result. Patients in double blind studies are given fake medications (what was perceived as real medication). The results were that many of the patients actually had real positive physical reactions and major illness reduction, even though no real treatment was administered.

Nocebo is the effect when instead of curing illness, people believe themselves into experiencing signs and symptoms of an illness. That's the ideology of a hypochondriac.

Whatever belief you hold in your subconscious mind, it will become your reality. This is why many scholars and philosophers teach, "If you can mold it in your mind then you can hold it in your hand." When you earnestly believe something to be true, your subconscious mind starts directing your actions to bring it to your reality.

WORDS ARE CONTAINERS

Every great communicator became that way through learning to effectively communicate. No one is born a great speaker. There are some who seem to be naturally talkative or naturally charismatic. Just because someone is speaking doesn't mean he or she is communicating effectively. Charisma alone won't make a person be a good communicator. The truth is most really great communication is learned behavior. Although some of our communication is learned by way of formal education, most of our communication skills have been learned through trial and error. We say or do something which produces some kind of result. If the result is good, we tend to repeat the behavior. If the result is not what we want, we try not to do that same thing again. Our problem is that we learn ways of getting subconscious desires met, even when they conflict with the conscious logical decision we have made.

Think of it this way. A little boy starts to like a little girl. He may do lots of annoying things like pull on her braids, stick his tongue out at her or event blow bubbles in his drink through a straw up his nose. He does all these things in an attempt to gain her attention. He usually will not get the type of attention he wants, but if he gets any attention, he'll try similar antics over and over again. He does these types of attention getters because he can do those same things with a buddy and they both laugh about it. He is trying to use what he has learned. It's not until he learns how to properly communicate his desires, in a way that she receives affectionately, that he gets the girl.

Humans crave contact and communication. We were designed to interact with one another. The ability to share ideas, past experiences and future plans sets us apart from any other creature on earth. Communication of our ideas and intent is the very foundation of reason and understanding. We receive information through our senses from a variety of sources, but no matter the source, it all has to pass through the filters in our mind. To make words come alive, we must first examine that initially, they are just information. In the process of how words work, we must explore what happens to the information we receive.

A phrase I have heard many people say, "information is power." What I've come to realize through studying communication is that words or information is not power, the use of information is power. The application of information is the influence or power of words. But information, in itself, is only empty words. There's a biblical reference which states "faith without works is dead" (James 2:17 NIV). Faith: a person's deeply embedded belief in the words that they've received is the truth on which they're basing their personal bias. But in itself that "word" or "information" that has been received is powerless until acted on by deed or by thought. It doesn't produce anything within the receivers' life without some sort of work behind the words.

In working with various educators, speakers and preachers, I have come to realize that many are speaking, but few are reaching. I found the same true in everyday people. We text, email, chat, Twitter, IM, blog, Facebook and even Instagram to send information, but it seldom really reaches the other person with the full intent or desired impact.

At one time the Internet was used primarily to share information for business, sales and education. Then came emails, message boards and blogs. These were the first social media. The blogs' message boards competed in the amount of content they could have and influence they could possess. The names of some new social media sound humorous.

"Users get a little Twitter when they become LinkedIn to Facebook, as they Flickr to an Active Contact."

The reality is "with nearly 260 million people using the web on a regular basis in the United States alone, using the Internet has become a mainstream social activity" (Singh, 2010). Social networking media has changed the way many people communicate. Some people argue that the information shared on Facebook, Twitter and various chats are dangerous to relationships, while others express the almost essential need for the detailed communication social media can provide. Both are true. The information shared can cause damage if not used in a responsible manner. Because social media has such a large following, there should be periodic education requirements for each user. The responsibility of everyone using a social networking activity should be focused on understanding how to present information and the impact of shared information.

Mehrabian, A., and Ferris, S.R. (1967), featured a study on communication which found that only 7% of our communication is the meaning in the words that are spoken; 38% has a paralinguistic meaning (how words are said); 55% of meaning is facial expression. This means that 93% of our communication cannot be stated in simple word format as when typing responses within social media like Facebook.

Gifted professional writers can challenge the study by means of the emotional responses their writings provoke. They cause the readers to visualize and draw specific conclusions. The average user of social media is not blessed with such a gift. The average user lacks the finesse to relay the details of emotional content that non-verbal communication can convey. Non-verbal communication, such as when a person has folded arms show a lack of willingness. When the listener stares at something other than the speaker, they are conveying a lack of concern for what is being said.

How the information is being shared is equally as important as what is being shared. Perhaps, it is even more important. Social media is a magnificent tool for quickly giving information to large groups of people at one time. The response to information on Facebook, Twitter or any other social media opens the door to the risk of an escalation of misinformation. After a statement is made, many of the responders seem to have a need to top the previous comments. In his book, The 7 Habits of Highly Effective People, Covey (1990) stated "to change ourselves effectively, we first had to change our perceptions" (p18). The goal is to provide a change of perception through understanding.

Some of the most profound results will come from small changes in the words you speak and listen to. There is a video clip (Gardner, 2010) on YouTube. It depicts a blind man who sits on a flattened cardboard box on the sidewalk of a street with heavy pedestrian traffic. He has a sign next to him that says, "I am blind. Please Help."

People walk by, but only a very few drop any coins to help him. As these coins hit the cardboard, he would feel around and gather them up and place them in a tin can he kept close to him. He would say thank you to each person who decided to help. One day a young woman dressed in business attire stops in front of him and picks up his sign. He feels her shoes as she stood there writing something on the sign. Without saying a word to him she just sets the sign down and walks away. Suddenly, people were beginning to drop money consistently. They would take time to place the money in the can and not just throw it on the cardboard.

The young lady came and stood in front of him. He touched her shoes and realized it was the same one who changed the sign. He asked her, "Miss, what did you do to my sign?" She said, "I said the same thing just in different words." The sign read: It's a beautiful day, and I can't see it.

THE FOCUS TO ACHIEVE -REACHING VS. TEACHING

In several of the youth programs I have helped facilitate, we played a game called "pass the secret." In this game, the originator reads in a whisper, a written secret to the first person in the group. Then that person has to tell the secret to the next person and so on until each person has heard the secret. Then the originator asks each person to tell the secret. Whoever says the original statement wins. The humorous part of the game is that very few people, if any, can recite the original secret, even when the information is relatively short. This is because each person remembers the information according to how the information was processed. Each of us has our own built-in filters. We don't just receive information and spit it back out. We filter every bit of information through our individual perceptions of that information.

The well-known explanation of our filters is accounted in a bible parable told by Jesus in Mark chapter 13:

"Listen! A farmer went out to plant some seeds. As he scattered them across his field, some seeds fell on a footpath, and the birds came and ate them. Other seeds fell on shallow soil with underlying rock. The seeds sprouted quickly because the soil was shallow. But the plants soon wilted under the hot sun, and since they didn't have deep roots, they died. Other seeds fell among thorns that grew up and choked out the tender plants. Still, other seeds fell on fertile soil, and they produced a crop that was thirty, sixty, and even a hundred times as much as had been planted! Anyone with ears to hear should listen and understand.

The disciples came to him and asked, "Why do you speak to the people in parables?

He replied, "Because the knowledge of the secrets of the kingdom of heaven has been given to you, but not to them. Whoever has, will be given more and they will have an abundance. Whoever does not have, even what they have will be taken from them. Jesus was letting his disciples know that not everyone will understand the concepts and principles He was teaching them. And the people who do understand can perceive the next level of teaching, but those who didn't understand the foundational principles, will not be able to perceive any higher teachings. Jesus went further to say, "This is why I speak to them in parables:

Though seeing, they do not see; though hearing, they do not hear or understand.

"Listen to what the parable of the sower means: When anyone hears the message about the kingdom and does not understand it, the evil one comes and snatches away what was placed in their heart. This is the seed sown along the path.

"The seed falling on rocky ground refers to someone who hears the word and at once receives it and is happy to get it. But since they don't have a deeper understanding, they last only a short time before the words they heard stop having an effect on them. When trouble or persecution comes because of the word, they quickly fall away.

"The seed falling among the thorns refers to someone who hears the word, but the worries of this life and the deceitfulness of running after wealth choke the word, making it unfruitful. But the seed falling on good soil refers to someone who hears the word and understands it. This is the one who produces a crop, yielding a hundred, sixty or thirty times more than what was first planted." (Mark 13 verse 3a-8, New Living Translation)

If we want people to get more out of what we are saying, then we need to guide them to get an understanding.

Like the seed falling on the footpath, some of the people don't really want to listen to what you have to say. We will speak to those people and hope they can take something from what we say to help in the future. There are some who want to hear what you have to tell them and are eager to implement change in their lives, but they have no depth, like the rocky soil. Then there are the people who want our words but haven't learned how to consistently apply sound wisdom long enough to permanently change their situations. This group has tremendous potential, but allow the daily activities to draw them back to old unproductive habits. These are the people who live among the thorns.

There is a small portion of the listeners who will listen intently, grasp the concepts and will diligently apply what they have learned until there is a permanent change and constant growth. This message is for each and every person who is willing to take the time to listen, understand and act on the lessons presented by people who are successful in that particular area.

When we are trying to reach people, we must take many things into consideration, but all of the properties of reaching people can be grouped into two categories: Speaker Preparation and Listener Preparation. The understanding of both is easier if you think of igniting a flame in the listener. When building a fire, we have to prepare the source of the flame to meet the condition of the items to be burned. It only takes a flame from one match to start a roaring fire on a dry day with no wind and a dry stack of paper that has had gasoline poured on it. But the flame has to be intense and relentless to start a damp log to burn on a misty day.

To build a fire in someone, there first has to be some kind of fire in you. To catch something on fire, the fire catalyst must already be in existence and/or the ability to spark a flame must already be there. We must get past the preconceived notions, the lack of focus, and even the unwillingness to hear so that we can get the wisdom that we have to share to be received by others.

INTERACTION OF THE SENSES AND THE MIND

The development of memory response is much more pronounced when multiple sensory triggers are applied. There were astonishing results when touch and music were utilized between a patient and Naomi Feil (2009). This prompted me to take a closer look at the incident. The founder of Validation Therapy, Feil, shares a breakthrough moment of communication with a patient, Mrs. G, who was diagnosed with Alzheimer's disease (AD) in 2000 and is virtually nonverbal. In the video, Feil (2009), a teacher and consultant on the care of those with AD, moves very close to Mrs. G and began to gently touch Mrs. G's cheeks. She later stated, "this is the way a mother stroke the cheeks of a baby."

Although it's not stated by name in Feil's interview, the process used is what I call "codifying." Codifying is a mental process used for tapping into repressed or difficult to recall memories. Vocabulary. com defines codify as "to arrange information in a logical order that others can follow." We attach emotional states to the memories of various events in our lives. A certain touch, fragrance, taste or even a song can take you to a memory of a specific time and place of bonded linked memories.

Feil draws upon Mrs. G's religious history and uses old church hymns to connect with Mrs. G. Initially, Naomi, while continuing to stroke Mrs. G's cheeks, sings the children's hymn, "Jesus Loves Me, This I know, for the Bible tells me so." Although Mrs. G does not join in the singing, she opens her eyes and focuses intently on Naomi's eyes; Mrs. G also begins to tap her hands with the rhythm of Naomi's singing onto Naomi's arms as well as the arms of the chair where she is sitting. At that point, Mrs. G was not responding verbally, yet her eyes remained fixed on Naomi's face. Then Naomi begins to sing "He's got the Whole World in His Hands." Mrs. G seems noticeably connected in the emotion of the song by the second verse. Mrs. G is so connected that she begins to sing along. As Mrs. G and Naomi come to the end of the song, Naomi asks Mrs. G if she feels safe and warm, with Jesus and Naomi. Mrs. G responds, "Yes!"

Feil (2009) makes a very profound statement in her explanation of communicating with people deteriorating due to Alzheimer's disease, "There is a desperate need for connection." This is a true statement for all people, not just the elderly. She further stated, "There is a longing for closeness." In Mrs. G's case, we see that certain types of touch are triggers which can be associated with memory patterns related to sight and sound. These connective triggers allow us to bridge the gaps of memories and those of modified thought processes.

Words as Energy

One of the most accepted scientific theories is the "Law of Conservation of Energy." The theory states that energy is neither created nor destroyed. Energy is just transformed from one type to another or is transmitted from one item to another. The energy of emotion can be transformed and conveyed through the energy of spoken words.

There are many theories and philosophies about the power of the spoken word. One very controversial theory is presented in Dr. Masaru Emoto's (1999) book "Messages from Water." Initially, Dr. Emoto's research led to a hypothesis that stated water takes on the "resonance" of the energy which is directed at it, such as through emotion. Emoto theorized the water is affected by words when spoken to. Congruently, he related the things which contain water will be affected according to how the water is affected.

His findings were done in two parts. One of the experiments was freezing water. By exposing water to good words, good music, and pure prayer, then freezing it, the frozen water produced amazing crystals (1999). The other experiment was with rice in water (O'Donnell, 2009). The results of both experiments are well documented, but the rice experiment details more of the intent of this book.

Emoto had placed equal amounts of rice in three glass beakers. He then poured water equally in sufficient amount to cover the rice each beaker. Next, he spoke to one beaker of rice saying, "Thank you", to the other he said "you're an idiot"; and the third beaker he absolutely ignored. Dr. Emoto did this for 30 days. After one month the beaker full of rice Dr. Emoto thanked had begun to ferment and gave off a sweet smelling aroma. The beaker of rice which had been called an idiot had turned black, but the most shocking was the beaker that had been ignored. It had begun to rot and grow mold. Emoto (1999) explained the results of the rice experiment to the energy expressed when the words are spoken.

Emoto's experiments have been attempted in many different environments: from clinical research labs to the living rooms in homes across the world. The results vary as much as the places where the experiments have been conducted. Many people have video documented their results on YouTube. Scientists and laypeople have not been able to replicate Emoto's exact results and have obtained a variety of personal experiences. Therefore, Emoto's experiment has been deemed to be a pseudoscience by many in the scientific community. As with any theory, there are people who do not accept Emoto's experiment because they feel it lacks sufficient experimental controls and that Emoto did not follow standard scientific methods for testing, documenting procedures, and gathering empirical data to receive the results being claimed.

Although his findings are not accepted as true scientific empirical data, the results confirm what most religions, philosophers and psychologists have noted for decades: Words have power. Moreover, Emoto's (1999; O'Donnell, 2009) experiments reveal to us there is a direct effect on physical matter by words that are emotionally charged. The term charged, in relation to both psychology and physical science means to move with vigorous force; to excite; to transfer energy or force. Several modern-day philosophers and religious leaders teach that words are containers. The theories vary concerning what goes into the containers, but they boil down to a few types of energy: emotion, thought and vibration. If this is true, then the emotion, thought and vibration of each person conducting the experiment has a direct influence on the results. This is why there are varied results of those who have performed "The Rice in Water experiment."

It is quite possible that when others have performed the experiment there may have been a major missing key: Thought with related emotion. When people speak or act, they operate in and convey the emotional energy they are drawing from. In other words, hurt people convey hurt; grateful people convey gratitude. The emotions and mental state of "hurt" are irritation, anger, bitterness, malice, loneliness, isolation and despair. The emotions and mental state of "gratitude" are satisfaction, contentment, peace, acceptance, and unity. Think of it this way. Ask anyone to explain how the words "Thank you" make them feel. "Thank you" from a person who was coerced or forced to say it, doesn't have the same power or effect as a "thank you" coming from a person whose heart filled with appreciation and gratitude.

Gratitude, thankfulness, or appreciation have an effect on the brain based on the article "The Grateful Bain" written by Dr. Alex Korb (2012). According to Korb, "Gratitude, particularly if practiced regularly, can keep you healthier and happier." His conclusion was based on the results of studies by Emmons & McCullough, 2003; Ng et al., 2012; Zhan et al., 2009, that shows how gratefulness can be a major factor to help promote better sleep, optimism and overall being happier.

One significant part of the gratitude research showed there is a clear distinction between truly having an appreciation of the positive aspects of your situation opposed to just viewing others as worse off than you. There are times when noticing the insufficiency of others can make you grateful for what you have, but it must go beyond the empathy for someone's bad situation. There must be a sense of the importance and value of the life circumstance you have been given.

The biochemical reason behind the effects of the feelings of gratitude is that the act of showing gratitude stimulates an active response in the brain which is associated with the release of the neurotransmitter dopamine. Dopamine commonly known as the "feel good" or "reward" neurotransmitter (Mandal, 2017). The great thing about the release of dopamine is that the brain says, "that made me happy, so let's do that thing again." Dopamine helps us to reinforce and search for things to be grateful for.

It is not always easy to remember to be grateful, particularly because the human brain is so adaptable. We easily get used to whatever comforts are around us. When was the last time you turned the key in your car's ignition and praised God for the miracle of the internal combustion engine?

There are numerous things we overlook or lack appreciation for. Floods or disasters like a hurricane prove to us that we should not take things like running water and electricity for granted. Even when we start getting a feeling of gratitude it does not seem to last. Usually, within a few days, you're back to fussing when the cashier takes more than 60 seconds to ring up 10 items at the store. The key is to purposely be grateful. In the cashier's case, be grateful that at least you were at the front of the line.

Inner Energy

Everything in the universe is made up of energy, including people. Thoughts and emotions also have and are made of an energy.

Negative thoughts and emotions have a low energy vibration, and so will drag down your vitality and the vibration of your entire being.

If your outer world may appear to be pretty gloomy, it is probably because the energy frequency of your emotions, mentality or spirit are affecting your physical world. Your outlook is being dragged down by negative thoughts and emotions inwardly resourced. This reduces your capacity to attract good things to you, as you can only attract things to you which are in alignment with your own vibration.

Conversely, positive thoughts and emotions emit a higher energy vibration, which is expressed in increased active vitality. Louise Hay (1984) stated "...if you don't have the thought, you won't have the feeling. And thoughts can be changed. Change the thought, and the feeling must go."

There seems like millions of books written about transforming your life by changing your thoughts. The general consensus is we have the ability to write what we want to say and do, we have the ability to do it, and we can even direct how other people will view it. If thoughts generate emotions and perceptions which in turn dictates our actions, as the person who is leading a conversation; facilitating a group discussion or a speaker presenting in front of thousands, our communication will influence the thoughts of others and in doing so, we affect their actions.

Getting Past the Filters

Children imagine in an active manner. When we were children we could easily visualize things within our minds. As children, we effortlessly mentally manipulated shapes and concepts, while checking and analyzing the scope of impacts of any changes made.

In the beginning, the cares of life hadn't tainted our view, but then we began to learn behaviors from the people around us and through experiences of our own. During our growing processes, we developed perception patterns concerning the meaning of words in relation to the context where we experienced them.

Literal meanings of words and phrases are considered denotative. Denotative words have an objective, specific and very literally precise meanings. An example of this is the typed words on this page are in black ink. Within this phrase, there is very little room, if any, for multiple meanings or interpretations. Denotative words are excellent for relaying information that is fact based and no conjecture is needed. Connotative words and phrases are usually sensory rich phrases. They are subjective, perception encompassing, and figurative. Emotions, feelings, beliefs, bias and assumptions are the base elements of connotative phrases.

In human speech, one of the most powerful, yet overlooked tools is accentuation for appropriateness of the occasion or situation. This skill capitalizes on the present cognitive state of the listener. The listener filters the words through the mental state created by both current and past personal experiences. Writing to accentuate takes real expertise, especially when using social media or texting.

An example of this is the phrase "I didn't say you are crazy." The meaning is completely left up to the interpretation of the reader when not accentuated properly. Even with the use of punctuation and capitalization, there is still room for misinterpretation. When spoken, there are opportunities for variances that better define the intent and meaning of the phrase that is not readily available within the confines of written text. Through simple voice modulation, word elongation and pause time the perception of the meaning of the phrase changes dramatically.

- I (pause) didn't say you are crazy. [Implies: Someone said you are crazy, but it wasn't me.]
- I didn't (pause) say you are crazy. [Implies: I said something, but it was not that you are crazy.]
- I didn't (elongated "say") you are crazy. [Implies: I may have text that you are crazy, but I never spoke it.]
- I didn't say (modulated up "you") are crazy. [Implies: I said someone was crazy, but I didn't say it was you.]

- I didn't say you (elongated "are") crazy. [Implies: I said you are acting crazy.]
- I didn't say you are (pause) crazy. [Implies: I said you may have some mental or emotional disorder, but not specifically crazy.]

These modifications made within speech change the basic perceived meaning of a phrase or sentence. In communication, even slight variations in the delivery of the message can change the perceived meaning of the message. True communication ensures that the information being shared is understood as it was intended. Understanding and interpretation become even more integral when we add: body language, facial expression, assumed point of reference, personal bias, and continuity of emotional expression.

We would think it is a joke, if a college student were to say to the professor "ain't nun yall gonna learn us nutin?" Well …in most places. Likewise, it would most definitely seem very inappropriate for a minister to giggle and chuckle throughout the eulogy of a fallen soldier. That kind of behavior is extremely incongruent with the emotional state of the event.

Our communication or words are containers. Knowledge and information are only the base ingredients for our communication mixture. Remember, Mehrabian's (1967) study concluded that 93% of our communication is not in a simple word format; therefore, we need to understand how perception in communication is affected by each of our senses.

When a baby is born the only comforts they understand are directly related to the experience they had in the mother's womb. Warmth, nourishment, mother's heartbeat and her voice are all familiar comforts. As the baby experiences hearing words and watching the interactions that associate a word to an action or object, the experience teaches them. This why a child raised in an English speaking home speaks English and a child from a Spanish speaking home speaks Spanish. As I watched my own children grow, I found that words don't teach, only experiences do. One might ask "how can I experience things that I have not or may never come into contact with?" The answer is to find the experiences from others through statements that are intensely descriptive, thought provoking, emotionally charged and that can be tied into something that the listener has previously experienced. The mind cannot differentiate a memory from a recent deeply perceived sensory rich image.

We can make our word containers so sensory rich with imagined sight, sound, taste, and touch that they will become filled with intense purpose and dynamic ability. The art of great communication is to relay thoughts and experiences to others. Those thoughts and experiences, in words, will become like fire (the flame of intense purpose and dynamic ability) for us and for those to whom we speak. The catalyst for a flame of communication is understanding how to effectively bridge the gap from the speaker to the listener through communication that follows multi-facet learning style communication.

The Ideal Learning Process

In the 1970s quite a few learning theories became famous in the education realm. Each of the theories focused on an individual's learning style. My definition of learning is the gaining or acquiring of new abilities, knowledge or skills. We go through different processes within our different age groups. As children we learn, through play, to recognize the shapes of objects and differentiate between colors; teenagers may learn to drive and improve their studying habits, and adults learn through their years of experience to solve complicated problems. For example, a brain surgeon must acquire high-level motor skills, medical knowledge along with good judgment skills before being considered qualified. This poses a significant challenge for the instructor to judge a person's capability to learn effectively and the application of that knowledge. This and the following chapters explain in-depth the psychology of learning.

Learning Theory

The theory of learning may be described as a group of principles educators and psychologists use to explain how people gain knowledge, skills, and attitudes. Numerous branches of the learning theory are explained in training programs to accelerate the process of learning. There are key concepts that apply to each individual's learning pattern, depth of training, desired outcomes, and the one's objective. When applied properly, learning principles that are derived from different theories can be very useful to instructors.

Many theories have surfaced over time attempting to explain how exactly people learn. Educators and psychologists aren't in complete agreement, but most agree that the learning process can be explained by two basic approaches: behaviorism and cognitive theory. Cognitive theory suggests that people have the capacity to process and organize information in their own mind. It is concerned less with visible behavior and more with the thought processes behind it. Behaviorism stresses that behavior is a learned process.

Children form their own behavioral patterns as they watch, learn and ultimately mimic, their siblings and parents. In the behaviorism theory the learning process there is a need to be given encouragement and positive reinforcement to the student by mentors to motivate the learner to gain or maintain success.

Types of Learners

There are various ways people absorb their surroundings to learn new things; some people try to either write it down or talk about it with someone close. Some hum along with the music or tap their feet. Some prefer reading the map, others read driving directions along the way. Some people might be more interested in taking an art class rather than join a gym. When someone is happy, they grin, but others jump with joy.

These behavioral patterns indicate some unique ways in which people choose to interact with their surroundings, and what people prefer reveals their learning style. Information is absorbed through our five senses; it's the only way we can effectively interact with the world around us and each of us process information in a unique way. Psychologists, researchers and educators have branded copious processing methods into broad categories which now are referred to as learning styles. There are basically three types of styles: Visual, Aural (Audio or Sound), and Kinesthetic. Although there are other categories, even predominant categories like taste, do exist, they generally fall into these major three. Our focus is on utilizing the senses to improve communication, assist individuals to maximize interaction and learning potential.

Sound Vibration and Resonance

Auditory learners. These types of learners prefer to hear the information. They can take advantage of lectures, web chats, group discussions, talking about things, or even music, and consume and retain new information quite effortlessly. Often individuals with this learning style process information by talking about it, instead of processing it first and then talking about it.

Aural learners can clearly understand what is happening by listening; the ability to see what's happening isn't as crucial. When they study, they prefer reading out loud and greatly benefit from repeating what they've learned verbally.

When a person says "thank you" with gracious intent the sound (vibration) energy produced by a voice is transferred to your ear through the movement of atomic particles. Sound is a pressure disturbance which moves through a medium in the form of mechanical waves (the distribution of energy through a medium by the transfer of energy from one particle to the next). When a force is exerted on an atom, it moves from its rest or equilibrium position and exerts a force on the adjacent particles. These adjacent particles are moved from their rest position and this continues throughout the medium.

This transfer of energy from one particle to the next is how sound travels through a medium. There are times the sound energy can disturb the cohesive bonds within an item, such as when a soprano hits a high pitch note to shatter a crystal glass or when a dentist uses a sonic resonator to dislodge plaque buildup from a patient's teeth.

The energy transfer sometimes has a good effect…music soothes the savage beast. There are several reasons sounds effect an individual's mood. Some sounds act as reminders or psychological triggers for a specific set of memories. The memory has a mood climate attached to it. The sound of a particular familiar song, perhaps "Jingle Bells" that was played during a time of a reoccurring happy family gathering can affect mood positively. Neuroscience has led the way into some fascinating advances in our understanding of the strong interrelationship between sound vibrations and emotions.

Sound waves enter through the outer ear and then travel through the ear canal to reach the eardrum. The eardrum then passes the vibrations through the ossicles (middle ear bones) into the cochlea (inner ear), where thousands of tiny hair cells convert the vibrations into electrical signals, which are then sent to the brain.

Based on a 2009 study performed by Treese at Lund University in Sweden, six psychological mechanisms were tracked through electrophysiological (EEG/ERP) and hemodynamic (fMRI) brain imaging techniques. This research showed specific brain patterns in relation to emotional responses to sound.

1. **Brain stem reflex:** When the acoustic characteristics of the sound (loud or dissonant) signal a "potentially important and urgent event", causing us to react on an instinctive level.

2. **Evaluative conditioning:** When an emotion is elicited by sound because we have heard it repeatedly in a certain setting, leading to an association between sound and setting.

3. **Emotional contagion:** When we perceive the emotion expressed by a piece of music: the music doesn't necessarily sound sad, but rather we recognize it as expressing sadness.

4. **Visual imagery:** When the structure of a piece of music makes us imagine certain scenes or sensations, such as a rising melody connecting with the sensation of moving upwards.

5. **Episodic memory:** Also known as the "Darling, they're playing our tune" phenomenon - when a particular sound or piece of music evokes a powerful memory.

6. **Music expectancy:** This is tied to our experiences with music: for instance, an unfamiliar variation on a standard note progression may cause feelings of surprise and curiosity.

Of these mechanisms, the author stated the first two are inborn reactions, the second two develop during the first few years of our lives, and the last two tend to be learned during childhood and later life. Certain sounds such as a gentle breeze, soft falling water and even a birdsong produce a neurological response which equates to the emotion of feeling safe or thoughts of peace. There are other sounds that produce a feeling of agitation, like the screeching noise of someone's nails across a chalkboard.

Some people say they enjoy listening to music when they work or study and they believe it helps them focus better. One of the most difficult tasks that I had a few years ago was to get my teenage children to do their homework without what I had thought was the distraction of listening to music. My teens, as well as many other students that I have mentored, have said that they could study and work better when they listened to music. To my surprise, they were right. There are frequencies and beats which cause real physiological and psychological stimulus responses that energize the brain activity of the listener.

The neurons of the brain communicating with each other causes patterns of electrical activity. There are a variety of emerging mechanisms and techniques which show promise in detecting and measuring brainwaves, but the currently accepted process used is the of the EEG (Electroencephalograph). The EEG shows that brainwaves are divided into four main categories: delta waves, theta waves, alpha waves, beta waves, and gamma waves.

There are many studies which reveal the frequency-to-brainwave patters as Beta– consciousness and reasoning wave. Beta brain waves are associated with the mental use when you concentrate on learning something or doing an activity which requires focus, also associated with being alert and active. The Beta (14-40Hz) wavelength is the normal waking consciousness and a heightened state of alertness, logic and critical reasoning.

In some relaxation therapy and meditation techniques, they are looked upon poorly, due to the association that beta waves are linked with over-thinking and worry. Beta brain waves are essential for effective conscious functioning, they also can translate into restlessness, stress and anxiety. (davinderojalla.com, How your brainwaves mold your success in life and biz; Jan 20, 2018).

Alpha– awakened deep relaxation wave. During deep relaxation and light meditation or when slipping into a daydream, alpha (7.5-14Hz) brain waves are present. Alpha wave state is optimal for directed imagination, visualization, memory, learning and mental programming. Many experts in the meditation field consider the "alpha wave" state as the inner voice. Alpha is also said to be the gateway to your subconscious mind and the beginning point of conscious awareness. The soft inner voice associated with intuition becomes clearer and more profound the closer you get to 7.5Hz, which is prime for guided imagery.

The mind becomes detached to sensory awareness as it shifts into alpha waves at 8-13 Hz. Many people are "in alpha" while watching a movie or television. During alpha, there is a kind of "hypnogogic" state. You may experience spontaneous mental imagery in relation to the images fed to your mind by the movie. The brain also produces alpha waves in that time frame just before you drift off to sleep and just before you wake up.

Theta– The light meditation and sleeping wave. At the beginning stage of sleep, alpha waves begin to disappear and are replaced by theta (4-7.5Hz) waves. The brain emits theta waves during light sleep and deep meditation. In the merging of alpha-theta waves, from 7Hz to 8Hz, there is an ideal range for mental programming and visualization. In this mental state, you can consciously create your reality because theta has a very subtle silent voice. During this frequency, your body is in deep relaxation, but you are aware of your surroundings. Theta is also, associated with REM (rapid eye movement) sleep. REM is the dream state where dreams occur and the mind does a kind of reboot.

Delta– The deep sleep wave. Very deep, transcendental meditation and dreamless sleep fully detached from awareness is the hallmark of the delta frequency. Delta (0.5-4Hz) waves are experienced in deep sleep and are the slowest of all the brainwave frequencies. The deep sleep allows the body to rest, heal, regenerate and restore homeostasis (normal physiological functions). Without delta, your body will not achieve its full restoration. There are many proponents that would suggest the delta wave unconscious experience is also, the gateway to the universal mind or the quietness where you can hear the voice of God through your inner man.

Gamma– The insight wave. Gamma wave is the fastest brainwave frequency. At above 40Hz, gamma directs simultaneous processing of information from different areas of the brain. The mind has to be quiet to access this rapid, yet subtle brainwave. For many years gamma brain waves were thought to be "spare brain noise", like white sound, as if it had no real pertinence. Recent research has shown gamma waves are associated with bursts of insight, universal love, altruism, and high-level information processing. Tibetan Buddhist monks have documented a correlation between gamma waves and transcendental states of consciousness.

Neurologists have also described a gamma brainwave that's thought to be involved with our sense of conscious awareness or expanded consciousness. The mystery still remains behind the origination of gamma waves because it is above the frequency of neuronal firing. We do know that by tapping into the deeper states of consciousness, you can open your subconscious mind and create your reality through modifying your precision. Understanding your different brain frequencies can help to find the right sounds to get a specific desired response or outcome by using behavioral modification techniques. These techniques help people control their brain waves to achieve better health, higher performance, and a more positive experience in life overall.

"The education of attention would be an education par excellence." William James.

TOUCH AND MOVEMENT

In my opinion, our sense of touch (sensation) is the most powerful accompaniment to any other modal of imagery. David Ginty, Ph.D., professor of neuroscience at John Hopkins, published a study in the December 22, 2011 issue of "Cell." He stated, "Touch is not yes or no; it's very rich, and now we're starting to understand how all those inputs are processed." Through thorough experimentation and study, Ginty and his team of neuroscientists shed light that the sense of touch is connected in the nervous system and skin. Ginty stated, "You can deflect a single hair on your arm and feel it, but how can you tell the difference between a raindrop, a light breeze or a poke of a stick?"

The phrase "don't touch that" is one of the most inhibiting sayings there is. When we were children it was our sense of touch which literally put us in touch with the world around us. We learn by handling and analyzing objects. As children, we called it playing. A person can gather much more information through their senses than they can perceptively understand. People can direct their attention to any of the objects present in your surroundings, but they cannot focus on (perceive) them all simultaneously. When we focus or attend to any particular sensation, we are aware of it. Perception requires awareness, sensation does not.

Our subconscious and our conscious mind both play a role with learning through physical touch and movement, many times the body quietly bypasses the conscious, logical mind and educates the subconscious mind on what to do. When someone touches something very hot, their body reacts to protect itself without the conscious mind being initially involved. People first learned to do certain things using the conscious, logical mind such as how to play an instrument or ride a bike, or how to catch a ball or even dance, but as soon as it is practiced your subconscious mind-body connection takes over. Doing those same things become effortless, to the point of it not even being a thought. In fact, many of the things we do, we can't really explain how it is that we do them. We just know we can. This body-to-subconscious connection is sometimes referred to as kinesthetic intelligence.

When a person operates in this manner, they are more likely to have great hand-eye coordination and will mostly have good control of their body movements with easily sustained skill. These types of learners communicate through touch and movement. They will also have a strong aptitude towards remembering and processing information through interacting and actively exploring the physical world around them with a hands-on approach.

The nerve receptors in our skin help us to identify objects and temperature. Some parts of our bodies have more and/or more refined receptors, such as our fingertips and parts of our face. These receptors help us identify objects from several expressions or modalities including vibration, pressure and temperature.

To focus or maintain concentration the kinesthetic learners usually do their best while touching and moving. The term kinesthetic is comprised of two functions: movement and touch (tactile). In other words, the kinesthetic learners must be doing something physically.

The kid in class who annoys the teacher by drawing pictures instead of taking notes in class. Sometimes they may want to take notes by drawing pictures, diagrams, or doodling. The goal for them is to be active while learning. When reading, they like to scan the material first, and then focus in on the details (get the big picture first). Although there are people who are primarily kinesthetic learners, we all learn from touch association and have kinesthetic memory.

The touch aspect of kinesthesiology took a major turn in the late 1970s as the "Human Potential Movement (HMP)" emerged. HMP set a fundamental framework where some psychotherapists, philosophers and religious teachers built a market around finding a therapeutic approach to coping and management mechanisms to people solve problems. A very significant mechanism was utilizing neuro-linguistic programming as part of their treatment practices.

The term neuro-linguistic programming (NLP) is said to be a neurological process in which language and behavioral patterns are learned through directed or programmed experiences. Richard Bandler and John Grinder, Ph.D. (1975), have developed NLP system as a means of altering specific behaviors through targeted goals. Although there isn't much formal scientific evidence to confirm Bandler and Grinder's claim to have used NLP as a form of psychotherapeutic treatment for behavioral health issues, the concepts and theories used as a communication model are very much supported with empirical data.

The NLP model suggests three main components:

1. Subjectivity - we experience the world through a subjective response representation of our five senses. (Suggested modifications of these sense-based subjective representations can prompt specific induced responses.)
2. Consciousness - Knowingly observed and the subconsciously observed sensory/linguistic input gained during the directed experience modification process.
3. Learning -Training the mind to re-sensor the thought and emotion of the initial sensory input by codifying or linking of the sensory input of touch, smell, taste or a sound to bonded memories to bring about specific emotional states in relation to linguistic representations.

Every day we experience sensations of pressure, temperature, or a chemical stimulant that can trigger an action potential to be sent along nerves to reach the brain where the information can be processed so we can feel the world around us.

Although each sense has its own method of initiating a neurological response in the brain, touch is our first learning tool. The sensation of warmth and vibration of its mothers' heartbeat and breathing are soothing to an infant, even before the ear has been fully developed. The connection the sensations of touch provide are usually more sensory verifiable than the other senses; as well as being easily trained to inter-link with the other senses.

SIGHT-VISION*SENSE AND PERCEPTION

In our daily lives, people rely on sight to perform most routine activities. The old phrases like, "eyes are the window to the soul" and "a picture says a thousand words" have had philosophers and researchers putting more emphasis on the study of sight and vision than any of the other senses. We, humans, are capable of complex color and depth perception. The technical side of the vision or sight system is made up of items, but the main sensory organ is the eye. The eye receives the physical input stimulus via light rays; which then converts or transduces the light rays into electrical impulses and chemical relays that are then interpreted by the brain to construct perceptual images.

The fundamental key is the brain has to interrupt the data it receives. Sometimes the brain can be tricked into accepting slightly skewed data as reality this is called illusion. The Oxford dictionary (2018) defines illusion as an instance of a wrong or misinterpreted perception of a sensory experience. Stripes embellish the surface to create the illusion of various wood-grain textures. Although there are some instances of malfunction of the optical system, most illusions are brain (thought) misinterpretations of the information relayed by the sense of sight. Bach stated, "an illusion is a mismatch between the immediate visual impression and the actual properties of the object" (as cited in Nierenberg, 2009, para. 4). The defining factor is not simply the mechanical side of sight.

Both vision and perception are used to relate to the world. There are pictures and/or visions we can purposely develop in our minds without ever physically seeing the item. We do this by painting word pictures. For example, let's talk about a dog. As soon as I said the word dog, your mind instantly goes to whatever dog you have had some sort of contact with. To change that picture, I must feed you details to form the picture I want you to perceive. As you mentally create this picture based on the words I give you, the dog becomes more and more real to you.

Can you see this dog?

Imagine a dog: This dog is medium sized, about two feet tall; he has soft slightly curly golden brown fur. He is groomed so the fur on his floppy ears and his short tail is longer than the fur on his body. His nose is black and his dark brown eyes are full of love. When you walk into the room, the dog kind of squats down, and wags his tail in a playful fashion. He almost looks as though he's smiling because he's happy to see you have come home. You now are visualizing a dog similar to a Wheaten Terrier.

Initially, you thought the dog would be reflective of whatever dog you remembered the most. But the more I described it, the clearer the dog became. When you added emotion to a clear image, the picture became more alive to you, almost like a recent memory.

The details of what was once just words, when imagined, became more defined and more alive. What each reader saw, in the beginning, was vague, separate and unique to each individual. After specific details were given, we all started seeing the same thing. Even to the point where it started an emotional response in each one of those based on the vision we were seeing in our individual minds. When we give examples, testify, or tell a story our aim is to help our listener to experience what we say, not to just hear our words.

Think of it this way. How would you feel if you bought some freshly cooked, golden brown fried chicken, but when you took a bite you see the meat is green? The meat could be fine, but you are not accustomed to having green chicken. Your taste buds play an important role in determining the four basic groups of taste: sweet, salty, sour, and bitter. Because we look at our food before eating, our eyes send signals to our brain well before our taste buds get the chance. Color is often the first element noticed in the appearance of food even before we taste it. We begin to associate certain tastes memories with colors of various food types from birth, and equate these colors to certain tastes and flavors throughout life. This can predetermine how the brain will interpret flavor.

Although many of us like to believe we are not easily deceived, our sense of taste is often fooled by our sense of sight. This is because humans have certain expectations of how food should look. When a food's color is different from what we expect, our brain tells us that it tastes different too. We use visual cues from color to identify and judge the quality and taste of what we eat.

For example, we may expect yellow pudding to have a banana or lemon flavor and red jelly beans to have a cherry or cinnamon flavor. In fresh foods, such as fruits and vegetables, we rely on the color to determine their level of ripeness and/or freshness. If the color of a food product does not match our expectations, we may perceive its taste and flavor differently. Some food companies use this psychological effect to their advantage.

In an article "How Color Affects Your Perception of Food (May 7, 2018)" to give the impression of a certain taste, flavor, or quality, food coloring or dyes are added to processed, packaged, and even fresh foods. Adding a red colorant to the skin of an apple, for example, may influence consumers into believing the apple is sweeter in taste. In a study published in the Journal of Food Science, researchers found people confused flavors when a drink did not have the appropriate color (How Color Affects Your Perception of Food (May 7, 2018). A cherry-flavored drink manipulated to be orange in color was thought to taste like an orange drink, and a cherry drink manipulated to be green in color was thought to taste like lime.

An example of the physical response to a remembered experience is what happens when we watch a person peel or bite into a lemon.

We start to salivate in preparation for the tart tastes, even though someone else is having the experience and not us.

Visual perceptions are used to enhance our overall experience of life; more specifically, they can be used to direct our physiological responses by influencing a remembered emotional state.

THE POWER OF A MADE-UP MIND

"Own the Experience, Before you Share It"

In presenting a dynamic awe empowered speech, there has to be a real connection between the presenter and what is being presented. The army spends hundreds of thousands of dollars to train noncommissioned officers (NCOs) to be instructors. In army courses on group instruction, soldiers are taught excellent mechanics of instruction and facilitation. By placing the major emphasis on communication and facilitation techniques, the trainer is missing one of the most profound parts involved in reaching people at a core level: being able to tap into their heartfelt convictions. I believe the importance of embracing the information or material being shared, is as important as the material itself. In most situations, it takes more than just learning the information on the material. We, as trainers, must create an environment and mental state conducive to receiving the full impact of what we have to say. We can help people improve their learning opportunity by providing a sensory rich experience they can see, hear and feel, but most important, we can make it relate to the emotional database which they already possess.

When you meditate on something long enough it becomes more real to you. Not only does it become more real to you, but you also become more certain in your thought process; more in depth, easily understood and fluently expressed; more of an actual experience.

The thought will begin to take on more power...fear begins to vanish and subsequently, authority comes forth. Sub-consciously you cause actions to happen. As stated before, words are containers. If you fill that container with power and authority when it is opened power and authority will come out. If your words are filled with being timid and fearful, your words will be weak...it won't have the burning resilience to overtake and change negative situations in your life or the lives of others.

Remember: The purpose of "Words Like Fire" is to inspire; to invoke an intellectual and emotional response. This book is meant to help bring an understanding of life-changing "empowered words" through the process of thought which shapes basic human behavior: information, meditation, revelation, application. The information received by whatever means it comes to you is just verified and unverified facts.

"Information" offers us facts, data or instructions in any medium or form. The way in which users interpret this information is based on the context: their business, the functions within their organization, and their working processes, customers and suppliers. Knowledge is the interpretation of information within its context. It is the result of perception, learning and reasoning. Knowledge gives users the power to make decisions and take effective actions. Although technical communicators often talk about providing information to users, they are in fact creating content that is tailored to their audience. Technical communicators who focus on user-centered writing have therefore already crossed the line from merely providing information to imparting knowledge" (Hughes, 2002, p.275-285).

When specific information becomes a burning desire, that information is beginning to go from being simple information to a revelation or enlightenment. We are not searching for an "Ah Ha" moment, but an "Ah-ha" moment. The point in which perception becomes your reality.

Earlier I made a reference to painting a picture... Keep in mind the purpose of making the impression clear and real is to ensure that an indelible pinpoint impact is made. If you don't fully believe the words you speak, you will convey doubt and weakness.

To get a good revelation of something there must be meditation. Scholars in various disciplines suggest meditation is everything from a reflective reading, to a trance state of consciousness. Meditation is the art of recapping imagining, ruminating on, constantly thinking about, or to focusing intently on a particular subject or object.

For simplicity let's think of meditation as painting a picture in the mind until it becomes the mind's reality. That's what everyday meditation means. It takes a picture (an idea) and uses all the body (hearing, smell, sight and touch) and the soul's resources (mind, will and emotions) to make one particular thing clear enough that it becomes a believed reality.

As details are added, to what begins as vague, the impression will start to become vivid and almost tangible. It will become more and more real, even to the point where it will start to put a demand for an emotional response toward each part of the impression or vision in the mind's eye.

The average person believes that they don't meditate. They believe meditation is a spiritual thing gurus from the Middle East do. There are many forms of meditation used worldwide. Some most common forms of meditation are Buddhist meditation, Zen meditation, transcendental meditation, mindfulness meditation, Taoist meditation, and Focused meditation. Meditation can be spiritual, but it's mostly simple focused thinking.

Focused (thinking) meditation is the practice of deliberately concentrating on something. For example, you could focus on a sound, an object, visualization, the controlled breathing, or specific movement to increase relaxation or awareness of a specific thing. Focused thinking can be used for stress reduction and to enhance personal or spiritual growth. The bottom line of any form of focused meditation is to teach our busy mind to become quiet, free from stress and anxiety by finding an inward place of calm reflection and contemplation to bring about change. Michael J. Baime (1999) once stated; in reference to positive thinking, "Meditation cultivates an emotional stability that allows the meditator to experience intense emotions fully while simultaneously maintaining perspective on them."

An everyday example of wrong meditation is: "Did I forget to get a cut stove off when I left the house? There is no one home to check. My pet could knock something over near the flames on the stove. Last year a house burned down and it could have been a stove fire. My house could be next." The Master Resilience Course developed for the US Army by the University of Pennsylvania calls this type of thinking catastrophizing, where one negative thought leads to another until the pattern becomes a downward spiral.

For many years there was no real way to measure the effects of meditation, except for the placebo effect. According to Hrobjartsson and Norup (2003), the placebo effect refers to the phenomenon in which people may experience some degree of medical recovery or benefit after receiving the administration of a placebo. A placebo is a substance with no known medical effects. Basically, a placebo is a fake treatment, for example, a sugar pill or colored sterile water. In some cases, the placebo produces a very real response. The placebo's effectiveness is based on the expectations of the patient; the more people expect the treatment to work, the more likely they are to exhibit a beneficial response. The key element here is the patient has become so intensely mentally focused on the expected results, there is a physical manifestation as if a real intervention had been made.

The medical field has virtual mountains of documentation showing similar benefits of various forms of "focused thinking" or "meditation." A Boston reporter, Melinda T. Willis wrote an article "Placebo Alters Brain Function" (2015) an account of a study performed by Dr. Andrew Leuchter (director of Adult Psychiatry at the UCLA Neuropsychiatric Institute and Hospital) had several very significant findings. Willis stated, "the study published in the American Journal of Psychiatry is the first of its kind to suggest that patients with major depression who receive placebos experience changes in brain function similar to changes caused by medication."

The double-blind study conducted by UCLA researchers used quantitative electroencephalography or QEEG imaging to look at brain activity in 51 patients who were assigned to receive either placebos or one of two antidepressant medications. After nine weeks, patients were classified as being medication responders, placebo responders, or non-responders to either medication or placebos.

"The placebo responders and the medication responders had changes in the same brain region," said Leuchter, lead author of the study and director of adult psychiatry at the UCLA Neuropsychiatric Institute and Hospital. "Placebo responders showed more activity in the prefrontal cortex while medication responders showed less activity. Additionally, the decrease in depression with the placebo was the same as the improvement with medication."

Some experts even believe the placebo effect accounts for as much as 100% of the efficacy of medication, according to Boston reporter Melinda T. Willis in her article Study: Placebo Alters Brain Function reported, Dr. Alexander Bodkin, director of the clinical psychopharmacology research program at McLean Hospital in Belmont, MA. "What we didn't expect is that people who get better on placebo would actually show changes in brain activity, as well," added Leuchter. "Placebo is commonly thought of as an inert treatment. It's supposed to be nothing."

The placebo effect happens when someone achieves a solid belief state by being convinced a physical intervention has taken place. The mind has accepted an imagined intervention. The results of having a convinced or made up mind are amazing. The body will make every attempt to adhere to the accepted beliefs that the mind has set as reality.

Now let's do some meditation.

Directed mental pictures are used in most aspects of our lives. Sometimes called "guided imagery" or "visualization." In this method of meditation, you form mental images of places or situations or things that match the emotional state you are trying to achieve. The term "imagery" is somewhat misleading because sight is only one of the senses being used. The best imagery will use all or at least as many senses as possible: sounds, smells, textures, and sights.

We often hear vivid stories and become caught up in the emotion of them. You may be lead through this process by an instructor or even some form of media. Many times, we don't perceive it as guided imagery. One day when I was grocery shopping, I strolled down the magazine and greeting card aisle. I began to realize that every piece of literature had one thing in common; they all used words and pictures to cause a specific emotional response. Guided imagery is the use of words or grouping of seemingly unrelated pictures to add specific details to one main thought process or mental picture. In other words, we build our vision of a thing by adding details until the full picture is clear. Advertisers use them all the time.

Some researchers believe the most powerful sense we can use is the kinesthetic sense for imagery. Although kinesthetic sense is thought of as touch, it also comprises the re-sensing (remembering or re-imagining) previous touch sensation.

An amazing clinical social worker and psychotherapist named Belleruth Naparstek (1994) presents what she deems is the three predominant principles of guided imagery as the mind-body connection, the altered state, and the locus of control. Now let's be clear, the mind-body connection is built on the foundational concepts that detailed images created in the mind can be closely linked as actual events. Moreover, the mind-body connection principle, according to Naparstek, leads us to believe; the mind can barely differentiate between a perceived experience and a true tangible experience. One example of this concept is: when we read a detailed recipe, we start to salivate. Our mind begins constructing sensory rich images of the food (how it looks, tastes and smells, possibly even the sounds of the food cooking or the feel of its texture as its being chewed). All of these thoughts cause the body to respond by generating saliva and an appetite.

Mental cues are linked to memories of an experience. The sensory connection has a more intense response when there is strong emotion attached to the experience. Based on my childhood memories, when I smell bread baking, it reminds me of spending holidays with my grandparents. The whole family would come over. Arguments were not allowed and every person there showed they cared. Just by simply thinking of the rolls baking I imagine smell, taste and texture of warm freshly baked rolls; but it also makes me feel loved and safe... and hungry, now that I am thinking of it. Sensory images are said to be "the true language of the body" (Naparstek, 1994). Sensory images are the only language the body understands instantly and responds without question.

The altered state is the second concept Naparstek (1994) taught. Naparstek conveyed that we are capable of more rapid and intense healing, growth, learning and performance through our brainwave activity and biochemistry shift. As our moods and cognition change, we are capable of being more intuitive and creative. In this Altered State, our body and our mind can accomplish things we couldn't do under normal circumstances. There are reports of a parent lifting a tree up which had fallen on a child, replacing our terror of a surgical procedure with a calming sense of safety and optimism, or abating a life-threatening histamine response to a bee sting. I'm not suggesting that we all go test the limits of our superpowers, but the ability to perform such feats lies dormant within us. Maybe someday we will learn to tap into this latent power.

Naparstek (1994) said, "We wander in and out of altered states all through the day, as a matter of course." "Sometimes it's not a conscious choice, and we drive past our exit on the highway. At best, the altered state is a state of relaxed focus, a kind of calm but energized alertness, a highly functional form of focused reverie. Attention is concentrated on one thing or on a very narrow band of things." Think of it this way: An ordinary altered state is that moment when we pinpoint focused and have a heightened sensitivity to the object of our attention, and our awareness of surrounding circumstances has faded away. During those events, we lose track of time and don't notice people talking to us.

Locus of control is the third principle offered by Naparstek. This is commonly known as the control factor and is defined as the sense or feeling of being in control. This one mental expression is the most prevalent toward total life management. The psychological principle is that the sense of being in control gives us mastery over the perceived environment as in the ability to tolerate pain, and stress, promotes optimism and self-esteem. When the mind-body connection, the altered state, and the locus of control is working in tandem, the communication and actions produced are effective through his or her ability to relay specific concepts to a given audience.

UNDERSTANDING DYNAMICS OF A GROUP

What is it that makes a perfectly rational individual suddenly become violent? What can a single person possibly do to provoke an entire room of innocent individuals to unite in a single violent purpose? Ausubel (1948), a historian and author, wrote: "A Parable That Inspires." This phrase refers to an individual who can influence others morality and actions. Reaching out to the humanity of people in times like these has the potential to calm a crowd down. Psychologists nowadays refer to this situation by creating a "cognitive dissonance." One of Ausubel's parables is a story about a Jewish tailor who decided to open a shop in an anti-Semitic part of town.

The youth in that area formed a gang and decided to harass the tailor by standing in front of his shop every day and yelling, "Jew! Jew!" to drive him out of the area.

This continued for quite a few days, and the tailor thought of a brilliant plan by deciding to use the stereotype that had formed against him to his advantage. He decided to reward every teenager standing outside his shop calling him a Jew with a dime.

The gang was taken back when the tailor approached them with a smile and told all of them he would reward every person who called him a Jew. They all shouted "Jew!" at once and the tailor gave each and every one of them a dime.

The gang returned the next day and began yelling "Jew!" again, the tailor came out of the shop and saw twice the number of teenagers than the day before, smiled widely and proceeded to reward them. They all happily left immediately.

On the third day, the tailor came out of the shop as soon as the gang arrived waited for them to chant "Jew!", and this time he apologized and said today he could only afford a nickel. The gang accepted the nickel somewhat less enthused and left after all a nickel was still a nickel.

This continued for two more days and each day there would be an addition to the gang. On the sixth day when the yelling started, he came out with an apologetic face and said that today he could only afford a single nickel. The crowd of teenagers began to protest, he said there was no way he could afford to pay them anymore and he would appreciate it if they all called him a Jew anyway. They spoke at once and said they would all be crazy to call the tailor a Jew with only a single nickel. They all left disappointed and stopped returning.

Plous (1993) related this parable to Festinger's (1957) selective perception studies which gave birth to the proposed "cognitive dissonance" theory. Plous explained, "According to the theory of cognitive dissonance, people are usually motivated to reduce or avoid psychological inconsistencies. In the absence of a sufficiently large payment, members of the gang could no longer justify behaving at variance with their objective (which was to upset the tailor, not to make him happy)."

We commonly call "cognitive inconsistencies" inner turmoil. When one has inner turmoil with a viewpoint previously held, a new line of reasoning has to be developed to ease it. In the case of the gang members, it meant not doing what they had initially purposed to do. The gang had intended to intimidate the tailor into leaving. This lends credence to understanding that crowd behavior can be modified when given targeted motivation to produce a specific emotional/thought state. By changing the gang member's motivation from anti-Semitic disruption to monetary reward, the tailor modified the gang's actions.

Just think, if over a few days a tailor who was targeted for an abusive attack, compelled them to avoid him, how can we move the groups in which we speak to produce a specific result? According to the Talmud, since the tongue is so influentially dangerous it is hidden from view, behind the mouth and teeth (which are referred to as 2 walls) so that it would not be misused. Eleven of the 43 sins recited during the Al Cheit on Yom Kippur are sins committed through speech. The Bible teaches that there are life and death in the power of the tongue (Proverbs 18:21).

Matthew 12:36-37 of The Living Bible (1971) states, "And I tell you this, that you must give account on Judgment Day for every idle word you speak. Your words "now" reflect your fate "then": either you will be justified by them or you will be condemned." In this text, the phrase "every idle word" means nonproductive or counterproductive communication. When you speak words you don't mean or believe those words are without power or authority. Such words can actually cause you to start unbelieving. An example of an "idle word" is saying "I am going to lose 10 pounds by next month" while you are eating a candy bar.

James 3:5 says "So also the tongue is a small member, yet it boasts of great things. How great a forest is set ablaze by such a small fire!" (Studylight, 2018). To help us understand riot psychologically, Gustav LeBon (1895), a French researcher, explained the behavior of people in groups as a decrease of overall individual intelligence and loss of their individual personality which results in a "Group or Crowd Mind."

The extended social identity model (ESIM) Stott (2004) is the currently prevailing approach in crowd behavior. ESIM states that we describe ourselves as unique people and by our affiliations with numerous groups. As members of a group, we shift our self-perception and identify ourselves more as a part of a faction and less as individuals. In times of intense emotions at a public platform, our group mind takes over our individual personality; we forget our personal constraints and any other behavioral boundaries society deems acceptable. When a riot erupts in a group of people, it resembles a forest fire. A small spark can ignite a pile of leaves somewhere in the forest, it quickly catches fire and moves onto the next bush or a tree. The fire then starts spreading rapidly, and even green trees that don't catch fire easily succumb to the overwhelming heat. The fire continues to gain intensity and rages on, becoming uncontrollable and consuming each and everything in its path.

When attempting to sway public opinion or a group mind, begin by trying to uncover the motivating factors. Once you bring that into perspective, the initial purpose of a group will reveal itself. Adjust your approach considering all the relevant factors; as mentioned earlier the key here is to connect with the group at an emotional level while keeping in mind their intent and what they wish to achieve.

An individual with the ability to communicate effectively needs to quickly decipher the cause of distress and tactfully address the situation in such a way that causes the group to second-guess their actions. Possibly, even redirect their aimless anger into doing something more purposeful.

Redirecting such intense emotions into purposeful behavior in times like these is also known as a controlled burn. A controlled burn doesn't put out the fire, it rather redirects its course to achieve a predetermined outcome. Often, firefighters use this technique to reduce further damage by redirecting it to a location it can no longer spread.

Since 2003, I've had the honor of working alongside several esteemed mentors who conduct programs for youth betterment. One program is through Center for Leadership Development, founded in 1977, as a response to what the community leaders of Indianapolis had identified as the main reasons why minority high school graduation and college entrance rates were on a dramatic decline. The reasons were various obstacles the youth faced to pursue academic excellence. Programs were developed based on five principles for success: development of character, excelling in education, effective leadership, career achievement, and community service. These five core values prepare and develop youth for the trials they will face in life along with preparing them for the highest level of academic achievement, successful careers and caring for the community. Through this formalized platform, accomplished African Americans, both women and men, would act as role models and give back to the community by becoming mentors to guide minority youth

One of the projects is a program for male 7th-10th graders where they discover the various skills, work ethic, and lifestyle choices required to achieve their goals. Participants learn a variety of techniques which could aid them in their personal life, their family, their community and the world as a whole. A major aspect of the program focused on learning how to deal with peer pressure and coping with the challenges faced in school life.

One way to get people on the same page is to have a few members communicate with an entire group to gain group consensus. In the project, a program was designed to train the youth to become leaders in their community; they would shout "one love" and everyone would respond. This exercise had a three-pronged effect. The first of which was to refocus the attention of the youth away from personal conversations and into a group mentality. The second intent of "One Love" was to declare that each member is a needed part of society through our loving solidarity. The third was more focused on the project name as a response, "Project MR." It gave a clear message that the purpose behind the gathering of a group of young men was unified male responsibility.

The facilitators also rehearsed the project's core characteristics at numerous times in each session; this empowered the young men with a guided imagery for becoming a good community leader.

Characteristics of a Responsible Man

- A responsible man not only loves himself but others as well
- Works on strengthening his mind body and soul

- Values education
- Nurtures his body
- Abstains from sexual activity until marriage
- Provides for his family
- Is a role model for other males
- Plans for his future
- Improves his community
- Respects women
- Demonstrates good character

The imagery is as crucial as the spoken words themselves. The facilitators interacted with the young men in numerous simulations. Whether in a story, a game, or discussion; each designed to be multisensory with embedded lessons. One of the most powerful lessons was declaring one's self-worth and inspiring respect by referring to all those present in the program as their surnames only. "Good morning, Mr. Smith, my name is Mr. Biggs."

This might seem like a small and insignificant change, but the psychological impact is huge because most people perceive "Mr." as a position of authority and power. "Mr." carries a connotation of predominance and using the last name (sir name) associated one with his whole lineage. In other words, this meant the person being addressed is worthy of respect and did not stand alone. By adding practical exercises to learning tasks facilitators and educators engaged the senses as well as the intellect. This type of self-actualization can be found to be very successful in any training or educational program. The power of respect and self-worth can dramatically affect how information source is received.

LAUGHTER

Another powerful tool in the learning process is humor. The body doesn't know the difference between real laughter and fake laughter and can achieve great benefits from both. An unknown author said, "Laughter is the best medicine. But if you're laughing without a reason, you need medicine." Although the author meant it as a joke, I totally disagree with the latter part of the statement. Laughter has been used to relieve stress and promote good health, both mentally and physically. The Bible actually states, "A cheerful heart is good medicine, but a broken spirit saps a person's strength." (Proverbs 17:22, NLT).

A hearty laugh can help to combat disease; is a practice that is gaining popularity in the medical field as a suitable form of alternative medicine. It was only a few years ago that there was very little empirical data covering the therapeutic value of laughter or its effects on mental and physical health. In recent years it has become common to find information about how laughter is related to stress and the immune system.

Stress alters the biochemistry of your brain by releasing the stress hormone cortisol. When you hold a negative thought in your mind, your body releases cortisol into your bloodstream, which weakens your immune system and inhibits the actions of your white blood cell. This makes you susceptible to infection. Cortisol is also the hormone that causes weight gain, especially in the abdominal area.

There are those who would argue: happy people do more of the positive things which promote good health and strong mental standing, but several studies on control groups have given new light to the effects of laughter. Laughter as therapy is based on the idea that a sense of humor is not only healthy but also, that a hearty laugh can physically make a person feel much better. When people feel better, they are more attentive; much more overall agreeable, which makes them ready to receive new insight. Charlie Chaplin said, "Laughter is the tonic, the relief, the surcease for pain."

The case of Norman Cousins (1979), is what started the laughter health movement. Diagnosed with ankylosing spondylitis, a collagen illness that attacks the connective tissues of the body, Cousins was often placed in the hospital as he tried to cope with his painful disease.

Out of interest, he began to read material about stress and how it can wear down one's immune system. Cousins read a book called "The Stress of Life" (Selye, 1956), in which Selye theorized that negative emotions cause stressful and harmful effects on the body. Through the information studied from the books and articles he read, Cousins then hypothesized that if the bad emotions do harmful things, then the good emotions should be helpful or healthful. At the time of his hospital visits, there was no cure or treatment for his disease. He decided to treat himself with laughter and found that 10 minutes of genuine belly laughter had an anesthetic effect and would allow him at least two hours of pain-free sleep. Henri de Mondeville (Tame, 2017) Stated, "Let the surgeon take care to regulate the whole regimen of the patient's life for joy and happiness, allowing his relatives and special friends to cheer him, and by having someone tell him jokes." This appears to be the motto that seemed to resonate in the life work of Cousins.

As this movement progressed on, a man by the name of Hunter 'Patch' Adams is noted as being one of the pioneers of the idea in formal laughter therapy. Many deem Adams as the originator of laughter therapy at the Gesundheit Institute in Virginia. Although laughter filled his later life, his beginning years were not filled with the laughter.

When Adams was young, his father ran the household in a strict military manner and as soldiers do, they were constantly moving. His family's frequent moves to diverse places, helped Adams learn to accept differences in people and to quickly make friends. He spent a lot of time with his mother and became very close to her. Unlike his father, who seemed to be always working, she gave him love and attention. It was his mother that fostered in him a desire to learn and a keen sense of humor. In school, Adams became known as the class clown. He played around and joked a lot in class because he got bored with what he thought was mundane education. It took a while, but he finally took interest in science and math.

After his father's death, Adams and his family moved to Northern Virginia to live with his uncle and aunt for a few months before moving to West Virginia a little later. In high school, he started to date his first girlfriend, Donna. They dated through high school, but the stress of the emotional roll coaster of his life caused him to have ulcers in his stomach. The medication used to treat him made him very sleepy most of the time during his senior year, which had a negative impact on his education. During his freshman year in college his girlfriend broke up with him, and his uncle committed suicide. Adams became dreadfully depressed and dropped out of college. Adams depression pushed him to become obsessed with suicide.

One day Adams confided in his mother that he had been trying to commit suicide and he needed to be checked into a mental hospital. His stay in the hospital changed Adams. He made friends with many of the patients. There was one patient who was suffering from depression due to loneliness. This made Adams look at his own life and realize he was loved by family and friends. Rumor has it this patient was the one who gave him the nickname Patch for Adams' passion for healing and patching up people with laughter.

Eventually, Adams got out of the hospital and decided to try to enroll again after working for a while. He entered pre-med school and three years later, he entered med school at the Medical College of Virginia. Adams maintained his love to go and visit the hospital patients. He enjoyed making them laugh by doing funny antics to amuse them. The University professors strongly disapproved of his behavior. They thought it did not reflect the seriousness of a potential medical provider nor did it show the professionalism expected of a doctoral level student.

Even though many of his colleagues didn't support his efforts, Adams saw his dream through to become a doctor. He decided that he wanted to build a hospital where he would be able to prove his methods in daily hands-on practice. After pulling together investors and tons of fundraising, his dream came to a culmination with the creation of the Gesundheit Institute.

Patch's theory on healing is definitely different. He believes that laughter is the best cure. Going to hospitals making people laugh and teaching regular doctors how to be funny for their patients, is the joy of his life. Patch has shown that he thinks "every doctor should be a heart specialist...a merry heart, that is" (Rutz 1999).

From the time he started his campaign to raise money for the Gesundheit Institute, he has written two books, Gesundheit: Good Health is a Laughing Matter and House Calls, he won the Institute of Noetic Sciences Award for Creative Altruism in 1994.

Although Hunter "Patch" Adams has served as a physician for 30 years and has received many awards, his true legacy is that he has been a clown for 40 years. Patch feels that the role of a clown and a physician are the same: "to elevate the possible and to relieve suffering." He says living in clown clothes is his gift to a world that he believes to be depressed, lonely, and lacking compassion. Adams has lived the life that a true physician longs for... to make people feel good. The only difference is his way is through medicine and laughter

In 1995, an Indian physician from Mumbai named Dr. Madan Kataria developed a technique referred to as "Laughter yoga" (Heerema, 2018). Dr. Kataria's laughter group met in a park. Initially, this first group of five people told jokes and funny stories to one another to stimulate laughter, but soon the group ran out of stories and jokes. The lack of new material leads Dr. Kataria to a decision to experiment with the idea of "laughter that was not based on any reason, but was contagious." His wife, who was a yoga instructor, added the idea of including breathing exercises, and thus laughter yoga was born.

Laughter yoga is a combination of laughter and "intentional" yoga style breathing, known as pranayama. In its most basic form, pranayama breathing is simply slow, deep and controlled breathing. The laughter classroom is set up like an exercise class. They begin by leading the members in fake laughter. In some classes, the facilitating instructor might use funny faces, childlike playfulness, and sometimes odd sounds to turn fake laughter into contagious real laughter. In laughter yoga, the objective is to incur approximately 15-20 minutes of uninterrupted laughter interspersed with occasional pranayama breathing exercise breaks.

Here is a major punchline…"Laughter Incorporated" stated, "laughter yoga is not only being taught in person but now is being taught via phone and Skype. Also, there are now more than 7000 laughter clubs in 70 different countries" (Heerma 2018).

The best way to get people to want to listen to you is to make them feel good. And what better way than to make them laugh!

HOW CHILDHOOD EXPERIENCES SHAPE YOUR OUTLOOK ON LIFE

The way a person perceives life is a complete reflection of what their childhood was like: their personal experiences, family values, education, friends, and the neighborhood they come from. A simpler term to understand these learned behavioral patterns is sometimes referred to as an iceberg. An iceberg is a massive chunk of ice that has broken free from the shore and flows with the current in the ocean. Most of the ice is submerged, with only about one-tenth visible. One cannot judge its size from just the tip, and that is where the expression "just the tip of the iceberg" originated. Therefore, when you look at a man, the part that is visible to you is not who he is, it is what he looks like.

When I was around 11 years old. I used to cut grass and do odd jobs around the neighborhood to earn money during the summer, which made me the kid who usually had money for candy and snacks. Because of a learned custom of my family, I always shared whatever I had. Normally this was sharing my toys, money, food, and candy on a regular basis with my neighbor friends next door. We were so close that, if I had something it was theirs too. One day I was helping them do their housework, so we could all go out and play. One of them had some potato chips and I asked if I could have some. But her response was "her boy, take some, you beg so much you make folks hate you." That phrase has stayed with me my whole life. To this day I find it hard to ask people for anything. People's past, the path they have been walking all their lives defines who they are. Many of us go around without the foggiest clue of why we think and react the way we do. Much of the conscious actions are dictated by our subconscious self-talk. Our inner voice gives us much of what we meditate on without ever realizing this communication ever exists.

Self-talk

A mental training consultant, Dr. Denis Waitley, suggested in the Psychology of Winning "it's not what you think that holds you back, it's what you think you are not" (1984). Martin (2018) said, "Most people don't realize it, but as we go about our daily lives we are constantly thinking about and interpreting the situations we find ourselves in. It's as though we have an internal voice inside our head that determines how we perceive every situation." This inner voice or self-talk involves everything that happens around us, as well as one's values, experiences, and knowledge. Whitbourne (2013) referred to this type of inner monologue as the equivalent of a sports narrator in a stadium. This inner commentary is used for the evaluation of one's actions and is good when the evaluations are self-validating or if it brings realistic constructive criticism. The problem occurs when this inner voice becomes overly critical and harsh.

A few years ago I learned that my inner voice or self-talk had a critical impact on my performance in weightlifting. Self-talk has been described as 'the key to cognitive control' (Bunker, Williams & Zinsser, 1993) and is usually referring to internal dialogue, including thought content and self-statements (Hardy, Jones, & Gould, 1998).

What I found was that when I went to the gym and thought I wasn't as big as the other guys and since I'm older my body won't be able to grow as they do…it didn't. As athletes, we are often taught to tune in to our bodies or their physical skills but are not taught to tune in to our mental skills. After studying the effects and applying the methods of positive thinking, I began to see an amazing change in my body.

It is generally accepted that negative self-talk is associated with low performance, whereas positive self-talk is associated with better performance. Positive self-talk may benefit an athlete by impacting their self-confidence, anxiety control, concentration and mood.

Technical or instructional self-statements can also be used to initiate appropriate actions (such as using a cue word to trigger a particular movement), and are often provided by the coach in the form of feedback. Neutral self-talk is often used by endurance athletes to dissociate from the rigors of their event.

Sometimes it may feel as though certain emotions are the cause of you thinking a particular way, but that is just because negative thoughts attract more negative thoughts. It is important to remember, thoughts are the creator of feelings and emotions. To improve how you feel you need to improve how you think.

When a person worries about something (dwells on the negative aspects of issues), the worrier's body responds as if those thoughts were a reality. Although the circumstances have not actually occurred, constantly having thoughts of bad things happening to you, will create negative emotions such as anger, fear or regret. These emotions then produce biochemical reactions in the body associated with stress and anxiety.

The Mayo Clinic Staff (2017) posed the question "is your glass half empty or is your glass half full" which plainly shows one's outlook on life as optimistic or pessimistic. Based on the answer, it sheds light on what kind of mentality the self-talk provides. People who consistently exhibit unrealistic negative self-talk, sometimes fall into a slow downward spiral. This self-defeating behavior actually changes the biology of the brain, which can be seen in brain scans, showing abnormal activity levels. Essential chemicals in the brain that carry signals between nerves go out of balance in depressed people. Your brain is the control center for your whole body. Remember the brain will act on what it believes.

The old saying "sticks and stones can break my bones, but words can never hurt me", is just one of those stories to toughen up the runt of the family. But the truth is words can destroy you if you internalize them. Negative emotional states brought about through dwelling on negative words have real physical attributes. Some physical symptoms are weakness, headaches, back pain, muscle aches, dizziness exhaustion and fatigue, sleeping problems, and change in appetite or weight.

I once saw a psychologist do a simple test which shows happy and stressful thoughts have a direct effect on a person's physical strength. He tells you to think deeply about a very happy situation. He asks you to describe it (where you were, colors, smells and most importantly how you felt). Then he has you to hold out your arm. As you hold out your arm and he tells you to resist him from pushing your arm down. He attempts to press down on your arm with two fingers.

It usually will not budge much. Then he has you to think about (relive) a time of a stressful situation, but when he presses down with his two fingers, he can push your arm down much farther than before. It is not his force being greater; it's your brain succumbing to the stressful situation you are reliving, making you weaker.

Signals from the brain tell your neurological system to increase or decrease your heart and breathing rate to identify the point and type of pain, allows you to speak and show emotion, makes you move and even controls how much you sweat. The brain directs the endocrine system to know which hormones to release or what enzyme to secrete and says where to send or to stop sending blood.

Our brain is the control center from which our whole body receives orders or messages to do almost all of the body's functions. The brain is the physical aspect of the mind. The mind is the function of processing that is conducted in the brain. The mind filters and processes information received through our senses or perceived senses. The mind will act on a sensory rich thought as if it were a currently received sense.

Through the learning of modification codifying one can train the mind to re-trigger the thoughts and emotions of the initial sensory input. A simple form of this technique is used in advertising. This technique has several applications, when used in advertising it allows businesses to stay competitive. Marketing psychologists are altering their approach and strategy by influencing what people think about the products they purchase. Such thought modification is the defining factor of whether a business or philanthropic organization fails or succeeds.

Visual learners

Tools such as charts, diagram, patterns, and maps are the best way for visual learners to consume information. They incline more towards the big picture and are very interested in designed layouts. People who have a visual learning style grasp new information quickly and efficiently. And when visual learners compile what they have learned, it would perfectly describe what they have learned.

Learning through reading and writing is what some of the visual learners prefer. As these activities are in a way, visual. This type of learning differs greatly from simply looking at things. The information is a text format, words are used instead of graphical representations. Rather than being spatial, it is linguistic. It shouldn't be surprising most famous academics belong to this category. Because graphics significantly differ from reading and writing, researchers are considering splitting this type of learning into two groups: Read/write learners and Visual Learners.

Taking detailed notes is a habit of both types of visual learners. Being able to see what they are learning is necessary for them, so they can visualize to jog their memory. Visual learners prefer creating colorful illustrations and imagery-rich language.

Translating written notes into graphical format allows graphical learners to recall intricate information rather easily. While read/write learners like to read or re-write their notes. They also find it quite helpful to summarize diagrams into written notes and making lists.

Methods for Accelerated Learning

To become a more effective and efficient learner, methods can be adopted to hone your brain. Most people prefer to get the most out of the limited time they have available. However, speedy learning is not all you should go for, other factors such as retention, recall, and transfer are also crucial. You should be able to remember the information you've learned and recalled it at a later time, along with utilizing it properly in a variety of relevant situations. Becoming an efficient and effective learner doesn't happen overnight.

The following practices can greatly improve your learning patterns if you adopt them into your lifestyle on a regular basis. Get the most out of your study time with regular practice.

Most people know basic tips like improving one's focus, avoiding cramming sessions, and structuring study time. But psychological research has proven that you can dramatically improve the efficiency with which you learn by doing the following:

Organize and structure. Group similar terms and concepts together or outline your notes accordingly. This makes it easier for your brain to store information.

Use mnemonic devices. Mnemonic devices are techniques used often by students to help them recall important information. This involves associating a term you want to remember with something you're familiar with. The mnemonics using positive imagery are the best. You can even come up with some sort of song, rhyme, or even a joke to help you recall a specific piece of information.

Elaborate and rehearse. To recall information, what you study needs to be encoded in your long-term memory. Elaborative rehearsal is an amazing encoding technique that is quite effective. An older version example of this technique is taking a key term and reading its textbook definition, studying and understanding it and then going into in-depth detail. Repeat this process a couple of times to make it second nature.

Connect new information to existing memories. When studying something that isn't familiar to you, a good place to start is relating the new information with something you already know. Establishing a connection between existing memories and new ideas greatly increases the chances of a person recalling newly learned information.

Visualize information. Many people prefer to visualize what they're studying. When studying, focus on the pictures and charts in your textbooks. If the book doesn't have any visual cues, create your own. Draw figures and charts as notes and use different colored highlighters to group your ideas.

Teach another person. Memory can be improved by reading study material aloud. Educators have also discovered when one person teaches new concepts to another it greatly enhances understanding, memory, and recall. Use this approach when studying by teaming up with a classmate and teaching each other concepts.

Pay attention to complicated information. Most have probably noticed it is easier to recall information at the start or end of a chapter. The order of information plays a crucial role when it comes to recalling pieces of information and is known as the serial positioning effect. Recalling information in the middle can be hard but it can be overcome by rehearsal. Another approach is to restructure the information in a way that makes it easier to recall. If a concept proves to be increasingly difficult, take extra time memorizing the information.

Keep learning new things. The simplest yet effective way to become a better learner is to keep learning. An article in Nature magazine Draganski reported in 2004 that people who learned to juggle increased the number of gray matter in the occipital lobes, the area of the brain that's associated with visual memory. When these particular individuals ceased practicing the new skill, the gray matter simply vanished. So to learn a new language, it is crucial to continue practicing to retain what you've understood and learned. This is referred to as a "use it or lose it" phenomenon which involves a process in the brain known as pruning. Pathways in your brain need to be maintained. If you want the information you've learned to stay, you have to keep practicing it. Otherwise, the brain will prune it away.

Gain practical experience. For a lot of people, typical learning involves textbooks, lectures, or conducting research. While reading new information and taking notes is important, actually putting fresh knowledge into practice is the best way to improve learning. To acquire a new ability or skill, gaining practical experience should be your focus. If it's a sport, train on a regular basis to maintain the skill level and muscle memory. If you are learning a new language, practice speaking with another person to improve it. Watch films in the language you're trying to learn to continue building your skill.

Instead of trying to remember something, look it up. Learning is an ever-growing process. Sometimes we forget something we've already learned for no reason. Instead of struggling to remember the item, try looking it up immediately as a better approach. Then write it down and say it. Remember, engaging more of your senses will make the information easier to recall.

Figure out your learning style. Another way to improve your learning effectiveness is to identify the learning habits that have worked for you so far. We have a better understanding of ourselves than anyone else, use this to your advantage and figure out the best way you retain new information. Everyone has their own specific formulae that work best for them; find your own.

Test yourself to boost learning. There is a general misconception that the more time we spend learning the more we'll learn. The information you've learned requires stimulation, the sooner after learning the better. As we learn new things, we store the knowledge. It's better to double check where you've stored it for later access. Testing yourself after learning something new is the best way to do so, it greatly aids your learning speed and recall ability.

Avoid multitasking. Busy people generally believe that those who can multitask have an edge over those who don't. Research has suggested multitasking actually makes your learning and cognitive skills less effective. Experiments conducted by Robert

Rogers and Stephen Monsell (1995) tested how fast subjects would complete the increasingly complicated tasks assigned. Those who were multitasking lost a significant amount of time switching back and forth, and those who completed the task one by one saved time. Switching back and forth caused errors and negligence that could have otherwise been avoided had the subject focused on one particular task. The best way to learn is to do one thing at a time. Immerse yourself into the task at hand to yield the encouraging results.

Effective learning is paramount in your endeavor to become a person who can influence others. The faster you grasp new concepts and absorb the details in your surroundings, the more quickly you can understand what you need to say to win the allegiance of the people around you.

Learning is not something you do every now and then; it's a lifestyle. It can take time to become an efficient learner, it can only be accelerated by your thirst and passion to acquire new knowledge. Establish habits which promote your specific learning style.

Adding Impact to Your Words

When you speak, your words must ignite passion in the hearts of your listeners. Your words must burn through their fear, insecurities, and delusions. In short, you must get through all the barriers they have built around themselves and reach their soul.

The art of persuasion is not saying whatever people want to hear, it's about portraying yourself as a credible person, and using your knowledge to influence the heart and minds of people. Knowing your audience is an added benefit which projects confidence and believing what you are saying is the key.

Believe it or not, Shakespeare himself invented hundreds of words, in most of our daily conversations we also speak Shakespeare as well speaking English. A popular myth led us to believe that an average person's vocabulary as compared to Shakespeare's is just one-third; his plays contain about thirty thousand words. Of course, all his plays combined contain more words but, speakers nowadays surely have twice the vocabulary Shakespeare did. An average educated individual and a mature English speaker know as many as 50,000 words.

Delivering Impact with Words

People who can others are usually articulate and skilled wordsmiths. These people speak the way George Walther, a communications authority, define as power talk. Power talkers possess the following unique characteristics: They use affirmative language and speak positively when they need something. They utilize their vast vocabulary using the right combination of words to deliver exactly the kind of impact they want Their choice of a word takes into account the person or people they're speaking to, the time and place, and how to get exactly what they want.

Let's take a look at an example. If you want an unmotivated employee to complete the analysis, instead of saying: "If you finish the analysis tonight, we'll all celebrate by going out for a drink." They say: "When you finish your analysis tonight, we'll all celebrate by going out for a drink."

Be Assertive

Persuasive people speak assertively. When talking about something, they describe their point of view, what they believe, and what they've achieved confidently and positively. Let's say we want to communicate with people, who we'll assume don't know you very well, don't know where you're coming from and what your underlying intentions are. When you speak, describe how you got to a certain conclusion, and provide the evidence to support your conclusion.

There was once a small town with a large factory which only recruited married men. One of the local women, we'll call her Ms. Dee, was angry about the recruitment of only married men and demanded to speak to the manager to find out why. Ms. Dee demanded to know, "Why do you hire only married men? Is it because you think women are weak, dumb, cantankerous or what?" The Factory Manager replied, "Not at all, Ma'am." "We want married men employees who are used to obeying orders, are accustomed to being shoved around, know how to keep their mouths shut and don't pout when I yell at them."

By sharing your beliefs with someone, you are effectively showing them a part of your soul. You are investing a part of yourself into the conversation, earning you trust points down the road. Sharing your history and achievements confidently and in a positive manner allows people to know you and then take the time to know the other person is the first step towards building trust. Only with trust can you persuade people.

Be Responsible

Good public speakers accept responsibility for their actions and avoid talking as victims. Instead of blaming others for their misfortunes when speaking, they show how they have taken control of the situations and accepted the responsibility for the outcome. They reshape the circumstances in which they find themselves through words; creating solutions on their feet.

Owning up to your positive deeds isn't a big deal, however, by owning up and taking responsibility for something that went wrong because of you or on your watch, can strengthen the audience's trust in you. It may be hard on you, but honesty defines your character. No matter how angry people may get, taking responsibility and fixing problems makes you someone others can believe in. The truth cannot remain hidden for long. Making excuses or redirect the blame because can obliterate the image you desire to be perceived.

Create a Win-Win Situation

What really sways people more than pure persuasion is a win-win situation. Using words to create a win-win solution out of a bad situation creates synergy and cooperation. Negotiating the best out of a bad situation is effectively a form of hand-to-hand combat, where words are used as weapons, respectfully of course. The art is turning the odds in your favor by highlighting key points which makes your argument superior to that of your competitor. This approach is hostile and talented persuaders don't utilize it. Instead, they mold a situation into one where both parties benefit from the situation.

Be Decisive

Skilled individuals that persuade people effortlessly speak decisively. Smart persuaders talk straight, instead of beating around the bush; they tend to get straight to the point and speak their minds; communicating exactly what they mean. Decisive speakers operate by projecting confidence and credibility. Being firm in your decisions and convictions is what people admire and look up to. When making a promise to do something decisive people don't only do it for the sake of the promise, but because they take pride in how well they can deliver on their word.

Show Integrity

Influencing people goes hand in hand with one's integrity. Power talkers project the sense of trustworthy soundness and avoid saying things that might make people question their honesty and sincerity. They also avoid unnecessary intensifiers. The overuse of intensifiers like: definitely, very, and surely promote thoughts of insincerity, if used numerous times in a conversation.

Many times, trust or belief comes into question with the misuse of simple adjectives. A politician weakens their position by overusing the word "very." Here are some examples of his common overuse: "I am going to have to work very, very hard to find a solution"; "I feel very, very deeply and very personal responsibility honor that has been given to me."

Being firm in your decisions and following through on your promises is a quality very few people possess. Integrity isn't something you sprout on occasion, it is a lifestyle. Be the type of person who says what he is and is what he says. People like to know who they are dealing with. Consistency earns trust and will cause people to believe you when you speak.

THE PRINCIPLES OF PERSUASION

People often are baffled by the incredible persuasiveness of certain individuals, and as a result, internally ponder the question "Can I do it as well?" After deeply studying some of the most influential personalities and leaders in the field of business, politics, social, and religious, there are crucial lessons we can learn. The following techniques are a result of in-depth research into the personality traits and mannerisms of influential personalities.

Basics

Persuasion isn't manipulation. Manipulation is the act of coercing people into doing something against their interests and if they were completely aware of the situation wouldn't do it willingly. Persuasion is the art of creating a win-win situation for all the parties involved. This includes getting people to do something that is in our best interest as well as theirs.

The line between persuasion and manipulation is quite thin, even blurred one can say. Persuasion involves gaining trust, showing integrity, and fulfilling one's word whereas manipulation is abusing another person as a means to an end. When people are manipulated they could eventually realize what happened; this is disastrous in a long-term relationship situation. On the other hand, when persuasion is utilized to create a win-win situation you not only create a great impression but form a lasting relationship.

Persuasion is about creating purposeful and lasting relationships with mutual respect for each other that is nurtured over a long time, whereas manipulation is short term. A manipulator disrespects a person, unethically takes advantage, and is simply used as a means for an end. So if you wish to persuade people you have to avoid manipulation and present the facts with conviction in a way which is easily understood.

Persuade only the persuadable. One can persuade anyone given the right conditions, context, and timing, but rarely in the short term should the nature of the persuasion be substantial. If your request is small, you can persuade a person fairly easily as compared.

A fine example is the target marketing of a political campaign. The marketing team of the campaign dedicates money and time to reaching a specific group to sway their opinion in order to decide the outcome of the vote during elections. This is more effective than general mass advertising, which usually results in wasted time and resources.

To successfully persuade someone the first step to identify the group of people who are susceptible to the specific topic you are about to broach. This includes those who will be sympathetic or at least open-minded about the topic and become the focal point of your energy and time.

Timing and context. The basis of persuading consists of the context for the people involved and the timing in which you are about to broach a topic. The context of a situation determines the standard of what's acceptable and what's not. For example, one wouldn't discuss a newly released movie while conducting a quarterly meeting. Timing relates to the current state of mind of the people involved. If a person is having a bad day and you force a conversation about your views and beliefs instead of comforting them, you will end up alienating them further.

As a rule of thumb, always read the room and the people in it. Observe if people are open to discussing the topic of interest, so you don't end up being an imposition. This is a tricky task because most people are polite and won't say anything when you start persuading. At this point, they will either disagree with you or just say what you want to hear to end the conversation. Apart from your failed approach, you also leave a negative impression that will make people close off to you the next time you're around. Work on reading the context of the situation and time your arguments accordingly.

First, create interest, then persuade. To persuade someone of something you should first build genuine interested in the topic. It must be tailored according to your listener. Most people are only interested in themselves or things pertaining to their family, security, love, money, or health. If it isn't something your listener could benefit from, they are likely to lose interest quickly.

Learning how to speak to someone solely about them, consistently, is a great place to start. People like talking about themselves when given the opportunity. This means…listen first! Use this to your advantage to get the conversation going, then when you speak you'll have their undivided attention.

Take time to build rapport. Rapport is a dynamic interrelationship made up of three essential components: attention, positivity, and coordination. Rapport is a source of confidence, which produces a willingness to be open to ideas and cooperate. The foundation of rapport is mutual respect. Some key elements in rapport building are developing confidence, cooperation, respect, dignity, and humanity with the parties you are engaging. Speak specifically of the things your listeners can relate to. When having a conversation note how people talk, what they talk about, the kind of examples they give to explain themselves. In short, try to figure out what makes them tick and you will know exactly what to do when trying to persuade.

In persuasion, positivity is used to add a sense of mutual friendliness and caring to foster the relationship. At the beginning of a relationship, there may be a fear of rejection. There may also be judgments made which inhibit an open and honest communication.

However, as trust develops, openness and honesty become more acceptable, as well as freedom for disagreement without damaging the relationship. Coordination refers to the level of predictability and understanding of the relationship between cross-cultural parties. As the relationship begins, awkwardness, confusion, and misunderstanding are common and even expected.

Reciprocity compels. Reciprocity is the act of repaying someone for something they have done for you; it can either be equal to what was done for you or more. It is a natural compulsion one feels when someone does something for them. It's basically a part of the evolutionary DNA which compels our species to help each other to survive.

The question is how you can use this to persuade people, and leverage reciprocity in your favor disproportionately. Take the people you meet regularly for example, at work or in your neighborhood, create a good rapport and show gestures of consideration to create a positive image for yourself. Then you can ask for a favor and they would be happy to oblige.

Persistence pays. A person who is willing to constantly ask for what he wants, and demonstrates his worth is quite effectively the most persuasive. Persistence with strategy can work wonders, but it takes an equal amount of effort as well.

Don't be annoying about it, consider the timing and context mentioned above to look for the perfect opportunity. Broaching the same topic several times a day is not only annoying but borders on harassment. Instead, casually touch the topic not more than once every two days, and judge the response of the listener, if he seems open to it go ahead and try to persuade and if they don't, back off for the time being.

Tasteful persistence is an impressive quality and is quite rare. When being persistent be prepared for people to verbally lash out and question your stance. Be well versed in what you are proposing, as you should have the answer for every question. Your aim is to persuade, but first you yourself must be convinced.

Compliment sincerely. Within our words, there is a hidden power that puts emotion in motion. "So also, the tongue is a small thing, but what enormous damage it can do. A tiny spark can set a great forest on fire" (James 3:5, NLT). Compliments are a great way to spark a trail of positivity wherever you may go. We are more likely to trust those for whom we have positive feelings, those who make us feel comfortable. Complimenting people on their achievements accomplishes that. Try offering sincere compliments often on the types of things people don't normally compliment about. It's quite possibly the easiest thing you can do to persuade others, it doesn't cost or require anything from you but a moment of consideration and thoughtfulness.

Once spoken our words scorch through feelings and emotions to set off a chain of events. In the end, it all comes down to how you treat the people around you, and how others perceive you. Try to create a reputation of openness, honesty, integrity and then maintain it. Treat everyone well and complement those around you to become the type of person people listen too.

Set expectations. Most of persuasion is about managing the expectation of others and having such a reputation that people trust your judgment. A manager who promises a boost in sales by 20% and delivers 30% are rewarded while the same manager promises 40% and accomplishes 35% is punished. To put it simply persuasion is about understating what others are expecting of you and over delivering on it.

If people expect the bare minimum of you and once you hand them more than they expected it immediately tips the scale in your favor. Your words and actions now hold the weight that was nonexistent before. Once you reach this level, you can begin creating an environment you desire around you and the way you want people to treat you. But remember to set realistic expectations for both what you deliver to others and what you want others to give you. Too much of either will greatly affect your credibility in a positive or negative manner, depending on the perception of the person being spoken to.

Don't assume. Never make the mistake of assuming in any aspect of your life; its equivalent to inviting disaster. Assuming someone has a need and providing a way to have that item isn't the way to go. Always offer value added in the area which the individual has expressed interest. In sales, quite a few sales representatives are known to hold back while offering products and services to the customer, with a baseless assumption that a particular customer doesn't have the interest or money to purchase it. Always offer what you can provide and then leave the decision to the person you are persuading.

When a person assumes something about another person, it is clear as day; their expressions give them away. Such an attitude has the potential of offending the individual at a level which might completely break off contact. The worst part is it won't end there because you just disrespected the person, and angry people talk. Whatever positive reputation you may have earned previously is bound to go down the drain.

Create scarcity. Human nature dictates one can never stay satisfied with what they have. We want any and everything we can get our hands on. Most times, we only want things just because other people own them, and should an item surface that is known to be scarce, it adds more value to it in our eyes; now we want it because not everyone can have it. We assign value to every article according to how we perceive them.

This aspect of human nature is continuously being exploited by multinational companies who go deep into the psychology of the human mind to create advertisement campaigns which compel people to make outrageous purchases.

On an individual basis, one can use this concept to persuade other people by creating value through scarcity. When persuading, don't be blunt about the scarcity, slowly build up the value of what you are offering. In the end, leave a small note regarding its scarcity; this should be enough to encourage the reaction you are looking for.

If you want somebody to want what you have, you have to make that object scarce, even if that object is yourself.

Create urgency. Now that you have established the scarcity of what you are offering, the next step is creating urgency. Scarcity accomplished one of the two-step processes. The first step was creating motivation to purchase the product; the second step is to compel action. This is achieved by instilling a sense of urgency to make people react right away.

The ideology behind this is that if a person is not motivated enough to take your offer now, they are unlikely to accept it in the future either. Creating urgency is one of the most valuable cards you could play when persuading people. When doing so, this second step is to be carried out the same way as step one, discreetly. When persuading don't be blunt about the urgency, slowly build up the value of what you are offering, in the end, mention its scarcity, this should be enough to encourage the reaction you are looking for.

Paint a picture with words. Another great tool of persuasion is effectively painting a picture with words. Describing what the experience is like, offering your own point of view. In short, you are trying to inspire the need for what you are offering. The most effective of salesmen know this and use it to the best of their ability to compel customers to purchase the product. Master your ability to paint an image for others, in their mind's eye, of a future experience you can provide for them.

Truth-tell. Most people sense when someone isn't telling the truth; they may not detect a lie, but the subconscious releases a feeling of uneasiness throughout the body. I'm sure most of you are aware of what I'm talking about. Sometimes effective persuasion is a product of being forthcoming and honest.

To persuade someone to tell things about them they themselves don't know and no one else is willing to tell them. Facing hard truths is one of the most meaningful, piercing, and life altering experiences in our lives, and if you happen to share that with someone it creates a bond unlike any other.

Once again note the context and time before broaching a sensitive subject, just because you know doesn't mean they want everyone else to know. Try to keep it a secret as if you've never heard of it. Make sure no one is around when speaking about such things and slowly ease it into the conversation. Be supportive about it; offer your perspective and do not make the mistake of assuming they don't know.

Building rapport. We like people we can relate to on a personal level, people who are like us. This extends well beyond our conscious mind into our unconscious mannerisms and tendencies. You can mirror and match behaviors, so others can feel more comfortable around you and open up to you. This is one way to build rapport. Another way is to show your qualities such as honesty, integrity, and trustworthiness. The better you show yourself as a person the more likely it is they will respond to your suggestions.

Personal Skills

In this section, we will talk about the personal skills one needs to hone to become an efficient persuader. These are basically personality traits that need to be focused on and developed. They are as follows:

Behavioral flexibility. Flexibility is one of the first traits an effective persuader should have. It is always the person who is most flexible that stays in control of a situation, and not the one who has the most power. Children are a fine example of effective persuaders. If parents don't put their foot down, their children would empty their bank accounts. They have a litany of behaviorisms at their disposal; they cry, pout, bargain, charm, and plead. The only responses parents muster up are either "no" or placing a condition on how they could get it, often through a good grade in math, for example. So the moral is the more flexible and creative you are with your approach in persuading, the more likely you are to succeed in this endeavor.

Learn to transfer energy. Over the years you have come across countless people. You are likely to have noticed some people are so charismatic they infuse us with energy whereas some drain us of it, and some can be downright painful to be around.

The people who are most persuasive learned how to transfer energy to others, to invigorate and motivate them. It can be as straightforward as making eye contact, laughter, touch, verbal responses filled with excitement, or even just listening intently. In doing so you won't only attract people towards you but, they themselves will be excited to be near you, hanging on to every word you say. You can then suggest your point of view and persuade them of whatever you have to offer.

Clear communication is key. If your topic is simple you should be able to make an 8th grader understand it. If you can't, the topic is too complicated. To persuade someone you should be able to simplify the complicated aspects so others can clearly comprehend what you are speaking about by highlighting aspects they can relate to.

If your object of persuasion seems confused, take a step back immediately and take a simpler approach. One way to do this is using a real-life example most of us go through every day. If you happen to know the people really well, take situations from their lives to create a custom-made example especially for them, things they care about.

It's advantageous to be prepared. When you start at a new job, your first plan of action is to get to know everyone around you and the mechanics of the relationships everyone has with each other in the office. This prepares you for situations that may develop in the future. Because different situations demand different approaches, knowing all the people around you and the relationship mechanics will accurately guide you when you take action. You will be more knowledgeable about how a person is likely to react to what you are about to do or say.

Let's say you intend to convince your boss for a raise; however, the only way you can tactically guide the conversation to the desired outcome is if you know how he or she thinks. Asking bluntly won't get you anywhere...except maybe unemployed. You have to be able to convince within the parameters that the office environment has set to not only keep your job but to get the raise.

Stay calm in case of conflict. Making emotionally charged decisions just makes things worse. Should a situation become sensitive don't make any rash decisions and speak as little as possible. If possible, leave the scene to clear your mind.

If getting away is not an option, make your best effort to detach yourself from the emotion in the situation. Think twice before speaking anything; every word that will come out of your mouth may make or break the prevailing situation. To become an effective persuader, master the art of detachment. When someone challenges our belief system, we tend to react defensively. Don't act on this instinct, instead, provide arguments supporting your statement.

Rather than getting all worked up over a minor altercation, take time to think things through and calm down. Then, lead the conflict into a win-win situation, and be the person people can trust to be fair when everyone else is edgy.

Redirect your anger purposefully. Most people aren't comfortable with any type of conflict. At the first sign, they would try to calm everyone down and try to switch the topic. Most of the time they would do anything required to prevent the situation from escalating.

This can be used in times when you are inappropriately challenged about your beliefs, or when your honesty is in question. Instead of taking offense and losing your temper, repurpose it and fuel your arguments in a cool manner. If you gradually escalate the tension, most people will back down.

However, if this is used regularly it will lose its effect. Use it sparingly, and never from a place of emotion or when you lose self-control. Pick your moments; if used at the right time, it can shift the situation in your favor.

Confidence. Confidence is a very attractive quality; there's nothing more intoxicating and compelling as a certainty. It will always be the person who's most confident and certain about what he says, who will be able to convince others.

People react positively to confidence, and when someone isn't certain about what they are saying it gives birth to doubt in other people. When trying to persuading someone uncertainty is not going to get you anywhere. It is only when you believe something to be right yourself that you'll be able to convince others into doing what's good for them, and maybe what is good for you as well. These situations need to be approached tactfully.

THE ART OF IMAGE MANAGEMENT

In your quest to become an efficient communicator every encounter with your audience, whether an individual or group, should leave a positive impression, a vibe that resonates well with the people around you the first impression is the last and it has scientific backing to it. Research has proven that it takes 1/10 of a second for someone to make up their minds and lock in the opinion they've made about you (First Impressions, Willis/Todorov, 2006).

The opinion initially formed is then used as a basis for all future interactions. This can be either good for you or bad depending on how the first meeting went. Although the impression you make is the premise interactions are built on, they can be altered by changing your outer appearance and how you choose to respond in that particular time and context.

Image management is all about highlighting your positive traits, and how you perceive situations that present themselves. Not everyone can make it happen on the first meeting, some people first like to get comfortable with people before opening up about themselves. This is why first impressions can be misleading.

People like to know as much as they can about a person; our Thirst for filling in the blanks fuels this desire. So, we subconsciously form an opinion about someone by considering factors based on past experiences with the individual. Because each person forms their own unique opinion, we don't have to worry about being perfect for others, but rather to protect our uniqueness by projecting our beliefs, ambitions, and the attitude with which we approach life.

History presents us with fine examples of power and talented individuals being underestimated because of the first impression they made. Both Neville Chamberlin and Winston Churchill didn't take Adolf Hitler seriously due to his posture, slick hair and his absurd mustache; this underestimation cost them dearly. Another example of such a mistake was made with Bill Gates. In the early days, he was underrated by his competitors and peers due to his unruly, geeky and nerd-like appearance. Now, look where he is.

People can easily set the record straight and show others who they truly are. However, the second meeting must be longer, about 6 to 8 minutes, to negate the impression you first left. Let's take a look at a few universally understood rules people to incorporate into their behavior which allows them to exude an aura of confidence. These habits make the kind of first impression that leaves people impressed.

Making a Legendary First Impression

The way a first impression is formed has been discussed at length above. The question is how you can use the first few moments of meeting someone to create a positive and lasting impression. Incorporating universally understood rules of interaction will set a firm base. Factors such as your body language, your appearance, your mannerisms, your demeanor, and the way you dress, all play a crucial role in setting your first impression.

To set the tone for all future interactions, decide on the kind of person you would like to be viewed as, and then stick to it. With every person you meet once a unique impression is formed, it is out of your hands. The only aspect you can control is the consistency of how you present yourself. Undoing a first impression can be very difficult because you approach from a position of weakness.

So, whether it is your social life or your career, it's crucial to learn how to leave a lasting, positive first impression. Read on and incorporate the following best practices in your life. They will definitely turn your life around.

Be Punctual

When meeting someone for the first time, agree to meet on a specific day and time. What matters in this setting is the very first promise you've made to that person. If they arrive on time and you're late, they won't be interested in how good an excuse you have. What they will remember for the foreseeable future is that you couldn't even keep your word on a matter as simple as arriving on time.

Give as much importance to your first impression as the party you are meeting. Plan ahead to arrive earlier than agreed upon allowing time for any unexpected delays. Arriving a few minutes early is much better than arriving even a second late. This first trait is the first and foremost that needs to be worked upon in a social and professional setting. People must believe you will be present exactly when you say you'd be.

Be Comfortable in your own Skin

The energy you bring into a relationship sets the tone for all future interactions, so if you are edgy and uncomfortable when meeting someone for the first time, you won't only set a weird atmosphere, but you may transfer those feelings of negativity to those around you. This can be disastrous for a first meeting; you may project feelings of distrust, not having the ability to control your emotions, and the lack of common courtesy to be polite.

On the other hand, if you are calm and collected, and confidently address your opinions and concerns, you come across as confident and down to earth. The other person can feel relaxed and at ease, creating a firm foundation for future meetings.

Presenting Yourself

Well-educated individuals and entrepreneurs understand that where genius exists there is also likely to be a touch of madness.

Physical appearance isn't as important as what you are capable of. However, such an unruly approach is suitable for established individuals who've made a significant reputation in their field. For those who are starting out with little to no network connections, appearance is the first aspect another person would focus on to fill in the basic blanks. Once you've built a rapport you can unleash who you really are as a person socially and what you are capable of professionally.

You don't have to imagine yourself as a model making an entrance to make a good impression. A calm, confident, well dressed and well-groomed individual who walks with purpose, and means business can do just as well. Appropriate self-presentation is the key to making a great and lasting impression.

As the saying goes, "A picture is worth a thousand words." Does your outlook create the impression you want to set? If people see you dressed poorly and the words you speak are captivating and inspirational, or perhaps the other way round, they may not trust you. Dressing appropriately for every occasion is an absolute must and what you wear should not conflict with who you are and how people perceive you.

Think about the most appropriate way to dress in a particular meeting or occasion. Is it a social gathering, a celebration, or a business dinner? Ask yourself what the evening is supposed to entail, who is hosting the event, and if there is a theme you must follow. These are just a few general aspects to consider when deciding on the most appropriate way to dress for an occasion.

In case of a social gathering, there are often some cultural dressing etiquettes which vary from country to country that one must adhere to. This is something that particularly requires your attention because by failing to act the part of an honorable guest, you may accidentally insult the host. When visiting a foreign country to attend any type of function, educate yourself regarding the country's norms and traditions beforehand.

Another factor is your grooming. Having a clean and tidy appearance is a must for most social and business gatherings. In gatherings such as this, do your best to stand out but never inappropriately, unless you are truly special in more ways than one. If you are having trouble calming down before a big event, appropriate presentation will help you feel like a part of the group, as if you really belong not to mention leaving a sound impression on anyone you meet.

Guard your Individuality

Fitting in is a good thing; at first. To be accepted into a group you must have traits that overlap with everyone else's. This is a great way to make people comfortable around you and can also prove to be your most powerful icebreaker. How long you keep that up defines who you are. If you blend into the extent you can't think for yourself anymore or begin to form a group mind, you will slowly lose your individuality. This not only hurts credibility personally but professionally, you may be viewed as gullible.

The best way to go about this is once you get into a group, project your individuality, what your ambitions are, how you perceive the world around you, and basically, everything that makes you unique. Share your individuality, celebrate it, set yourself apart from the crowd and yet a unique part of it.

Smile! By: Lt. Col. Thomas Hundley

Reflecting on my childhood summers in Mississippi always brings back wonderful memories for me. Whether it was riding our bikes all over town, or playing Little League Baseball at the park, or going fishing every morning or just playing outside all day long, the summer months were very happy times. But the thing that makes me smile the most is remembering the big glass of Kool-Aid that was waiting for us after each event. I know why that red pitcher on Kool-Aid commercials always had a smile on its face. Yes, I now know it involved too much sugar, but I don›t think I have ever seen a kid frown after drinking a glass of my favorite summertime treat. No matter which flavor was served, orange, grape, lemon or cherry, you can best believe this kid always had a Kool-Aid smile (Hundley, 2008).

Keeping a smile on your face and maintaining eye contact with others, subconsciously makes them smile as well. As the saying goes, smile and the world smiles with you. Use this to exude a positive aura around you, it will make you appear more approachable and a pleasant person to talk too. Not only does it put the other person at ease, but makes for a pleasant first impression. However, there is such a thing as overdoing it. If you smile too much or force a smile you might come across as smarmy and insincere, or even sometimes perceived as a pushover.

Being Confident and Open

When you first meet someone new, your appearance, how you carry yourself and your body language says a lot more about you than your words do. The micro gestures in your facial expressions and body language give everything away to a trained eye. To project all the right aspects with your body language, stay conscious of what you do when speaking or just standing there. To project confidence stand tall, make eye contact, smile, and shake hands firmly. This would put both you and the person you are meeting at ease.

Most people get slightly nervous when meeting someone for the first time. Over time and regular exposure, people learn to hide their nervous habits such as jittery nerves, sweaty palms, etc. By staying aware of how you act around your peers, you can keep a check on them. Once you gain control of these habits you will feel more confident and look forward to every situation or meeting that presents itself to you.

Figure out a Person's Temperament with Small Talk

At a social gathering talking about yourself before someone asks, is considered to be rude. Conversations are about give and take; if you've just met someone for the first time it's better to begin with small talk. You can take various approaches to create a connection with the person you are conversing with. Begin by finding a connection with the host. Talk about the people you know are here, and if there is someone noteworthy whom you both should meet. Once the ball starts rolling, you could ask them about their profession or if they are here with someone or if they having a good time.

As this back and forth goes on, note how the person behaves towards you, is he comfortable and at ease? Does he give you his/her complete attention? There are various verbal and body language cues you can keep an eye on to discover that person's mindset. Should a meeting be related to business, researching a little about that person can go a long way to create a good impression.

Dig around to discover what their hobbies are like. Does he golf? What kinds of cuisines does he like? Such questions will enable you to set the perfect venue for the meeting, a familiar environment for you because you planned for it, and familiar for the other person because it is their object of interest.

Building rapport will be easier if you have some background info on the person. Knowing the kind of things a person enjoys tells a lot about them after all. You can use this to your advantage and find points you can press to persuade them. For example quoting their favorite political leader to make a point, if it applies to your conversation. Personalize every aspect of the meeting to the person you are meeting. Whether or not you take this approach the other person is likely to, and your lack of preparation can offend the other party.

Remain Positive

The attitude with which you approach your life is quite apparent in the way you carry yourself, how you dress, and what you say. Moreover, in social and professional gatherings the attitude with which you walk into the room says it all. So always wear an aura of positivity around you because it can attract positive things in your life. This way people will be more open and relaxed around you.

People usually appreciate a fresh air of positivity in this negative world we live in. Your attitude projects everything about you. Even when facing criticism or when feeling nervous, use this negative energy and mold it into positivity; if you don't, this sense of unease will slowly grow. Face such situations with confidence and clear any misunderstanding or misconceptions with a positive attitude. Not only does it show character but shows everyone you can keep your cool in situations that are challenging for most if not all people.

Always try to learn everything entailed in a situation you find yourself in. By being well informed it allows your mind to build a strategy when your beliefs and views are challenged, which is what most people will do as you gain prominence. Strive to gain a better understanding of everything a meeting involves so you don't feel surprised by anything someone throws at you. This will enable you to maintain an upbeat attitude and contribute your fair share to the meeting positively.

Be Attentive and Courteous

What separates us from animals is our ability to show compassion to fellow human beings, and how we treat the people we meet defines who we are. Being on your best behavior goes a long way. No matter how unruly the crowd gets, always keep your cool. It shows your character in a positive light.

The type of gathering you attend does not matter; always show good manners. It shows where you come from and that you value the person before you. Showing politeness proves that you are capable of selflessness. Being attentive to others creates an unspoken bond that other people values above all else. After all, it's not every day you meet people who hang on your every word. So be that person. Offer compliments and positive reinforcement during the conversation to show that you are actually listening. Correct them if they are wrong, but judge beforehand how that person is likely to react.

Last but not least, either place your phone on silent or switch it off entirely. Nothing is more annoying than a ringing bell during a conversation. Not only is it extremely rude, if you choose to receive the call it can destroy your first impression. When meeting someone for the first time, they deserve your complete attention; anything less and you would quite possibly lose any shred of interest they may have in you.

How to Use Body Language

Body language is as crucial a part of interaction as well as your facial expressions. Controlling it is a skill that can be mastered with regular exposure in social and professional gatherings. The following are basic guidelines to aid you in getting your fundamentals straight. After which it all depends on you; pick up positive attitudes from others, and apply it to yourself. Constant exposure is the key.

- Face another person squarely in the face.
- Hold eye contact.
- Adopt an open posture.
- Lean forward.
- Touch.

Face the other person squarely in the face. As mentioned in the previous section your attitude says everything about you and is enough for most people to decide whether they would like to get to know you. Your face is quite an effective gauge to judge your emotional state; it is the kind of attitude you are projecting, and how you feel about meeting someone. Expression reading is done by all socially active individuals; it is basically a go-to approach. You cannot control the fact people will always be reading you; what they read, however, is in your hands.

Show that you are interested in the other person by directly looking at them, to let them know they have your complete attention. Slightly tilt your head to any side you feel comfortable with to show you feel relaxed in their presence. Now you also have to show interest in what the other person is saying. This can be pleasantly achieved by arching your eyebrows as if you're thinking about what the person is saying to you. As you understand each point the person makes, nod in acknowledgment to show you either agree or understand them.

The above can be achieved only when a person is in a relaxed state, keeping track of what is being said, the context in which it's being said, and deducing why the person cared to share that particular story in the first place. If you are thinking that is a lot of things to keep track of, don't; it is our second nature to capture details. The flow of information may seem overwhelming at first, but you eventually learn to sort the flow of information and categorize it accordingly. The key to being proficient at this is exposure to social settings.

If you have trouble relaxing at any given time you can exercise being aware of your surroundings, where you are, why you are there, who is present, and the atmosphere of the room. This little exercise locks you into the present moment, and the knowledge of your surroundings relaxes you. In this mindful exercise, the amount of detail you take from your surroundings is up to you; you don't have to count the number of blinds on the windows, for example. Just enough details to create an appropriate replica of the situation in your mind's eye.

There are various other ways to relax. What works for one may not work for another, so find the one technique that suits you best; learn the best way to quickly use it in situations that makes you uneasy. Once you've mastered the ability to stay relaxed at all times you can confidently approach social situations and face people with an impressive attitude.

We all trust and listen to people who are open about what they feel, how they express themselves by animating their facial expressions. The people who we feel are open with us we trust more easily than people who keep a rigid face. We have an entire sub-section on why smiling is our most powerful tool, so apply that here as well. A smile is a direct way of saying I like you and I'm happy with your presence; it conveys a subliminal message of care and trust while projecting confidence and warmth.

Always ensure that your message matches your facial expressions and body language. Mixed messages can weaken your influence over other people.

Adopt an open posture. A person's posture can tell a lot about their personality traits, their level of confidence, their status, how receptive they are to others, and much more to the trained eye. There are two broad categories of posture, namely Open and Closed. The names of these categories are self-explanatory; an open posture is about carrying yourself in a way that puts people at ease and makes them feel comfortable around you. Some people say very little with words and say everything with their posture. Once again, exposure to social situations is the key to mastering this.

A closed posture will basically give out signals that will prevent people from approaching you. A closed posture is reflected in a clenched fist and folded arms. Not only does this put others on edge and make them very uncomfortable, but it can also prove damaging for your reputation. Some cultures view this as preparation for rejection or for violent action.

So to master the art that is positive body language, adopt an open posture. That is standing or sitting with your arms primarily at your side and hands unclenched. Your chest, abdomen and extremities should be easily seen in the open position. You never know what kind of opportunity may present itself. This posture is a warm invitation to everyone around you to approach and speak freely, greatly increasing the likelihood of you winning them over.

Calero and Nierenberg wrote about research conducted on human behavior. They discovered that after a negotiation concluded the parties involved would unbutton their coats, uncross their arms and legs, sit forward in their chairs instead of leaning back, and move their chairs closer to the other side of the table. The researcher named these practices as a "Getting together cluster", and this was always accompanied by words that stressed on the positivity of the negotiations.

This study demonstrated that after the tense environment of high-level business meetings with high stakes concluded, all the participants involved assumed a more open posture that washed away all the hostility prior to negotiations. This was followed by kind words that strengthened the bond between the two parties by focusing on the positive aspects both were gaining.

Let us take this very example from a different approach, if after the negotiations both parties had adopted a closed posture like keeping their coats buttoned, crossing their arms, leaning back in their chairs uninterested, and sitting further away from each other, they would have appeared more defensive and negative.

The negotiation may have left them unsatisfied, or perhaps they did not get the desired outcome, whatever the underlying feelings may be, acting out in such a manner is downright rude, especially after signing an agreement. Such an attitude would most definitely hurt the long-term relationship between the two parties.

Enough about the posture you should maintain, let us now talk about what you can do with this knowledge to read the people you are trying to persuade. Suppose you broach a topic and are trying to sell it to a group of people. Notice the changes in their posture; if they still maintain an open posture it would indicate they are open to hearing what you have to say. If they cross their arms or legs they may be rejecting your idea or point of view. If they clench their fists, you may have really offended them.

A way a person stands and walks is also crucial, if the stance is upright it projects pride, confidence, and competence. Slumped shoulders, on the other hand, communicate uncertainty, vulnerability, and uneasiness. Your walk also conveys various types of messages; long strides, and a purposeful walk are usually goal oriented whereas people who drag their feet may not have a sense of direction in their lives. This is, of course, broadly speaking; there is an entire science of postures and you might want to read it to get more insight into the topic.

Reading postures is a great persuading tactic, which acts as a meter that shows how well you are doing with a person. It lets you know if what you are saying is getting through to the person or not.

Maintain eye contact. How often do you struggle to hold eye contact with someone you are having a conversation? During an entire length of the conversation, people seem to be staring everywhere except the eyes of the person they are speaking with. This is a big "no-no" for people who want to make a good first impression.

To project confidence, sincerity, interest, and empathy, creating and holding eye contact during a conversation is necessary. This shows the other people that you find them appealing. Not holding eye contact or quickly breaking it once you make it, not makes you seem insincere, but you inevitably end up disrespecting that person by not looking at them.

There are various types of eye contact; some warm and inviting as well as cold and hostile. Depending on the situation you find yourself, and the emotions involved dictate the type of eye contact a person makes. But once again it's something a person can control. With a healthy exposure to social events, where there are cocktails of emotions flying around, you can learn to keep your cool and decide for how long to look at another person, instead of reacting and losing control.

Facial expressions and eye contact both fluctuate to the level of emotions we are feeling. If you feel relaxed you will maintain a soft and warm eye contact. If you your emotions are going haywire, your face will show it. The key is emotional control; if you want to persuade other people, you shouldn't sweat the small stuff; let it slide over you the way a drop of water slides off a leaf. Letting negative emotions fester can lead to a constant state of anxiety. This will result in a mixture of emotions on your face. Not only would you send mixed messages but you may seem untrustworthy to the other party.

So try to assume the relaxation exercise mentioned in this section. Look at people square in the face, then purposely relax your facial expressions when feeling nervous or edgy. Plus do your best to maintain a warm and inviting eye contact to put the other person at ease. Doing so will help you persuade people easily.

Lean forward. The fourth aspect of your body language that you should project when interacting with someone is leaning forward when speaking to them. This projects confidence and shows that you are confident and aren't afraid to speak your mind or share your point of view. This creates a great impression if you are meeting someone for the very first time. Leaning forward also shows you are interested in what the other person has to say and if you happen to be planning something you are saying that they are 100% onboard.

The socially acceptable way to lean forward is either by being comfortably seated or standing in a relaxed manner, and then leaning in the direction of the person who you are speaking with. If you are seated, place your hands on your knees or clasp them lightly. What you are trying to do here is putting the other person at ease with your body language. Leaning forward provides positive reinforcement to the person who's sharing their ideas with you ensuring that you value what is being said and are ready to take action.

However, if you lean back when someone says something worthwhile, you are loudly saying with your body language that disagrees and rejects their point of view. Remember another person is sharing their point of view, something they have put a lot of thought into, and had the courage to share it. Leaning back with your arms crossed or clasped like a church steeple show indifference and is considered rude. This creates a barrier between you and that person for good because you showed them what they are worth to you which in their eyes amounted to nothing.

In your efforts to becoming a sound persuader, such an attitude can permanently damage your rapport with that person and with those who were present at that time. Not only would it spread negativity, but will put other people on guard around you.

Touch. The most socially acceptable contact between two individuals is a handshake. It is used in every social and business setting. A firm handshake is the most positive and safest way to convey warmth and friendliness to another person. Walk up to a person and offer to shake their hand as you introduce yourself. However, remember to keep the handshake brief and firm and ensure not to apply too much pressure. The handshake should only last between 2-5 seconds; anything longer borders on invading private space, and is not appreciated.

A firm handshake with a warm smile creates a great first impression; you not only project confidence but a rare quality of taking initiative. It shows you are outgoing and open and eager to meet other people. However, a limp handshake suggests you are disinterested in that person in more than one way. Everyone hates a limp handshake and women, in particular, loathe it. Not only are you indifferent to their presence but also to what they have to say. Always make sure your hand is dry and your handshake firm.

There are other types of handshakes which are disliked, and using them in social and professional situation leaves a very questionable impression. To ensure that you don't make the mistake of not knowing the impression you left, these handshakes are named as follow:

I'm dominant. Offering to shake a hand with your palm facing downwards is equivalent to showing dominance over another person. When you place your palm downwards, the other person has to forcibly place his palm upwards, as if submitting to that person. It can be appropriate in business or social situations where the environment is hostile and you clearly have an upper hand. But generally, this type of handshake is inappropriate and highly disliked.

If you find yourself to be the recipient of a dominant handshake, you can step to the left to force both hands to naturally assume a straight posture, evening the playing field in the process.

When you are trying to make a good first impression your approach to the handshake should be modest. Trying to dominate someone when meeting them for the first time will annoy them, make you appear arrogant and insensitive to the context of the meeting.

Bone Crusher. Along the lines of a dominant handshake is another type of handshake known as the bone crusher. If you've ever been the recipient of this handshake, you understand this is no joke. Not only is it very uncomfortable but quite painful as well.

Your grip should not be tighter than when you grip a door handle. In addition to that, you can do what most people do by trying to match the grip strength of the other person when shaking hands. On a side note, shake the hands of the elderly with a loose grip.

If ever in a bone-crushing predicament, make a comment on it like, "wow, that's quite a grip you got there." The person is likely to back off. If you are the type that gives a bone-crushing handshake, cease immediately. It may work with other jocks, but normal people just might begin avoiding you as the first thing you do when you meet them is cause them pain.

Limp fish. As discussed above, the handshake that is on the other end of the spectrum is the limp handshake. Limply shaking someone's hand suggests you are uncertain about yourself, nervous, and uninvolved. Having a limp handshake doesn't matter if it's unintentional; it creates the same impression as a limp/ nonexistent one. It can affect your position in a social circle or a professional setting and may also be a reason why you are not getting the promotion you have your eyes on. The reason that promotion hasn't happened could possibly be due to your superiors thinking you cannot handle the job.

Just fingers. Limp handshake however isn't the end of the spectrum; yes, there is something worse than that namely a "just fingers" handshake. It is almost never intentional, but sometimes handshakes miss the mark. You don't have to feel too embarrassed as the other person feels just as awkward as you. Nevertheless, it is always a good idea to laugh it off and put both of you at ease.

You can avoid falling into this trap by making sure the webbed part between your thumb and forefinger connects with the person you are shaking hands with, before grasping onto their hand.

Always be mindful of the person you're meeting; such a mistake would only occur if you aren't focused on the person you are meeting. This might suggest you aren't serious about the meeting, which might hurt the impression you want to make along with disrespecting the other person.

Cold, clammy, and sweaty. If you happen to be the nervous type when meeting new people, it most likely results in one of the following; cold, sweaty, or clammy hands. That makes the nervous person more nervous, although you may feel as if the particular issue is out of your control, it probably isn't. There are various ways to lessen the tangible impact of your nervous state.

Carry a handkerchief or a paper towel in your pocket, when you start feeling the side effects of your nervousness you can discreetly wipe your hands in your pocket whenever you get the chance. To avoid cold hands try not to hold cold drinks in your right hand when meeting people. Or quickly slipping into the washroom to dry and warm your hands using a hot air dryer.

This will provide you with a boost of confidence, allowing you to be more forward and open with the people you meet. It's not the cold or sweaty hands that are the problem, it's what it causes; the lack of confidence and the reluctance to meet people because of your nervous habits. You may not be able to control sweaty or cold hands, but what you are in control of is how you treat the people around you, and that is what really matters. Never let your nervous habits get in the way of interacting with people.

The double-hander. This type of handshake is a sign of ultimate respect to someone you know personally; there are situations where it can be appropriate, like meeting your father at church or your grandparents. Using the double-handed handshake with someone you first met may seem overly intimate or personal, which puts most people you have just met immediately on guard.

It isn't socially acceptable to show such a grand gesture to someone you have just met; give the due respect and try your best not to overdo it. The goal is to keep the environment light, and a double-handed handshake isn't the way to go. It is best to reserve this particular handshake for people who are close to you.

The long handshake. We have all experienced that long uncomfortable handshake, where the other person just refuses to let go. If at all possible, don't be that person. What is the point of holding a handshake long after the initial introductions are over? Other than making the other person feel uncomfortable and trapped.

The length of a socially acceptable handshake when meeting someone for the first time should be no longer than 2-5 seconds. And definitely no longer than the introduction phase. When faced with such a handshake, people stop focusing on you or what you're saying; they just stand there waiting for the awkward handshake to be over.

Putting people at ease is your goal when meeting someone for the first and shaking someone's hand this way makes them edgy. If you wish to leave a great first impression, avoid shaking a hand like this at all costs.

Eye contact. Making eye contact during a handshake is a sign of confidence and being forthcoming. When someone shakes a hand without making eye contact, one can't help but wonder what that person has to hide. This automatically creates a wall between people, and it's a characteristic which makes a person difficult to trust.

If unable to make eye contact due to social anxiety or perhaps being nervous, try focusing on the spot between the eyes so you give an appearance of making eye contact. Making eye contact in a comfortable and relaxed manner is the most important part of interacting with others.

Not making eye contact shows disinterest in a person and borderlines on being disrespectful. You also give an impression that you aren't a very honest or open person. This will most definitely hurt the impression you are trying to make.

The miss. As the name suggests, this type of handshake is clumsy and the hands don't quite come together. One either misses the other person's hands entirely or just ends up shaking the tip of the fingers. This happens more often than you might think and can be awkward for both the people involved.

It's best to just laugh it off, pull back and shake the hand again. Don't forget to make eye contact, if you do then you would have dropped the ball entirely. Continue with the introductions, or whatever you had planned to do when you met that person without the bad handshake making things unnecessarily awkward. It is an honest mistake that can happen to anyone.

Applying Persuasion Techniques

At this point in the book, we have learned a great deal about the dynamics of adding fire to your words, convincing people with your point of view, and persuading them to do things they otherwise would never do. I'm sure what surprised you most are the variety of aspects one must first learn, consider it in every situation, practice it with constant exposure to social and professional gatherings, and ultimately mastering the arsenal of techniques one has at their disposal.

If you weren't aware of the level of personal development required to achieve this, you do now. A considerable amount of work needs to be done to achieve finesse in adding weight to your words. You have learned in-depth about how to build a reputation, rapport, credibility, and the positive body language that needs to be maintained. While reading this chapter you should keep them all in your mind as we will learn to apply these techniques.

Intensifying and Downplaying

When persuading there are two completely opposite strategies you can employ to achieve the desired results, they are: intensification and downplaying. Either can be used depending on the situation or parts of both highlight specific parts of the conversation and downplaying another to achieve the desired result.

Intensify. Intensification is highlighting a specific aspect to make it more significant for those who are listening. Having the ability to draw attention to a specific part of conversation allows you to take various approaches to gain results. You can either divert their attention away from a mistake you made or share the significance of something important. There are three ways you can use intensification; the first is repetition, the second is association and the third is composition.

As you read about these three ways, you will notice how the marketers apply this very same concept to their campaigns and commercials. As these techniques aren't only effective at just getting the message across but also in delivering precisely the context in which the consumer should take it. Imagine doing the same thing when trying to persuade someone, only in this context the products you are selling are your ideas and plans.

Repetition. When having a casual conversation with someone you are trying to persuade, you can share your ideas bit by bit. If you do it all at once, you are more likely to leave the person confused. Persuasion of something significant is a slow process and requires time. Leaving a breadcrumb trail that leads to your goal is a sure way of persuasion.

As you leave breadcrumbs, the points you make must be repeated several times from different perspectives to reinforce the particular idea or image in their heads. The listener would be more likely to remember it, these breadcrumb trails will later help when you are actually trying to persuade them, the grand finale.

On the other hand, when something is repeated enough times, listeners are quite likely to accept a statement as the truth. Once your small suggestions are accepted as true, you would have laid the groundwork to persuade them.

This concept is presented clearly through advertising campaigns seen on television and in every form of media. Keywords are used in great repetition to tell consumers why a product or service is a good idea. By ingraining the subject product into the consumer's mind, it is more likely to be remembered when out shopping.

Simple association. This technique is a very subtle one and the ultimate tool of persuasion if you can master it. This technique specifically creates a connection between your concepts to another idea to which the listener is already emotionally connected. You can appeal to both the negative and positive aspects with this technique, which one you use is entirely dependent on the context of the situation.

A fine example of this technique is convincing someone to keep a job, by associating the loss of a job with bills, family comfort, or loss of home. This won't only make them question their decision, but will make them stay if they don't have it all figured out. Another example would be to persuade someone to accept a delegated task with no tangible rewards by associating a sense of accomplishment and pride to the reason they have been chosen, such as their competence and intelligence.

In commercials you must have witnessed how lifestyle products, branded clothes, and cosmetics are associated with beautiful people that don't have a care in the world when they use the product, giving them all the happiness that they have been craving.

This particular technique can be practiced and honed as a skill; very few utilize it to all its merits. To persuade with this technique you first have to know something about the person you have in mind. Get to know their mindset, what they like and dislike to successfully associate your concepts to the ideas they hold dear.

Composition. This strategy involves using descriptions to create mental images for the listener by delivering your idea in two parts. First hinting at the more positive and desirable aspect of implementing your idea, and then comparing it with a negative, unwanted aspect that is sure to befall them should they fail to implement your idea. Basically, you are trying to make your options sound, not only better but logical and allowing the listener to come to this same conclusion.

This concept is much like the before and after commercials you see on TV. A fine example would be a commercial of a waterproof paint, where the homeowner was suffering from dripping ceilings, and paint peeling off, but as soon as they use the new and improved paint all their problems magically disappear.

Your skill with the association technique will greatly compliment this one. Both can go hand in hand to persuade your listener into doing what you want them to. Emotional tug plays a substantial part in Composition as well.

Downplay

On the other end of the spectrum of intensification, is downplay. This is an opposite strategy as compared to intensification. Here your aim is to direct the attention away from some aspects of a particular situation. There are three tools that are also the opposite of those discussed in intensification which are at your disposal for downplaying: the first is diversion, the second is omission, and the third is confusion.

Diversion. This is one of the most basic distraction techniques one can use. When you realize you are flowing down a conversation path which could soon be turned against you, you can divert the conversation to another aspect or feature of an argument. A fine example of diversion would be when asking your manager to allow you to work from home, upon this request the manager will bring up the issue of not being able to supervise you.

Instead of letting your manager dwell on that issue you divert it the positive side by saying you know how the work is done, working from home can be more productive without distractions, and the time you save on commuting can be put into work. This will make your manager look good in the long term, when you are completing projects faster and much more efficiently.

Omission. This technique is exactly as the name suggests, when persuading someone it is not healthy to reveal everything about your ideas until a firm relationship is established. Some aspects might make the idea unacceptable to the listener. You should deliberately leave out aspects that could be deal breakers to building a positive and long-term relationship.

Consider what their reaction will be once they find out. If it's something insignificant they won't even bother bringing it up, but if it was something that may have crossed a boundary of some sort, you won't only have broken their trust but may end all discussions. It is usually a judgment call and how you choose to handle things with the situation you are presented.

Confusion. This particular persuasion tactic isn't the most ethical but it is widely used none the less. If this particular technique isn't your cup of tea, then you can at least learn what it's all about so you can be aware when someone else is trying to pull it off on you.

This technique is about establishing yourself as an expert on a complex topic. If a group is discussing a topic, about which you hold in-depth knowledge you can override the conversation, by bringing up the more interesting aspects and discussing its intricate details. In doing so, you take the conversation to a more interesting level establishing you as the expert on the topic.

Knowing a topic inside and out gives you the upper hand in social and business situations. We discussed how important knowledge and the many ways you can become an effective learner. All of which were leading up to this point. Knowledge makes you confident when speaking; leaving an impression that impresses all.

The first aspect is the demonstration of knowledge; the other aspect is creating confusion, and then removing it, effectively establishing yourself as an authority on the topic. This technique has multiple uses that can come in handy in various situations, diverting a conflict, suppressing the anger of someone, or simply covering up your or another person's mistake.

Persuasion is a skill that can be mastered, but how one uses it is a personal decision. It all comes down to the values and ethics an individual holds dear, which determines how they plan to use the persuasion techniques at their disposal.

Sequence and Steps Persuasion

Alan Monroe, a Professor of Speech at Purdue University, in the 1930s, created a detailed list of key points or prerequisites to persuading another person later written in his book "Principles of Speech." (Monroe, A. H. (1943).

The modified overview of Monroe's Motivated Sequence is as follows: 1. Capturing Attention 2. Need 3. Satisfaction 4. Visualization 5. Compelling Action

Capturing attention. In order for someone to listen to the argument you've prepared, one must first be able to get their attention. When conversing with someone you are trying to persuade, you have around 5 seconds to capture, hold, and engage his or her attention. Otherwise, they tend to lose focus and look for something else that can engage them. Attention can be captured in a number of ways; the following are a few guidelines that may help you do so successfully.

- Call out his or her name with a sense of urgency using, a tone that suggests you want to say something important. This immediately captures their attention and in most cases, they would listen to what you have to say intently.

- Another way to capture attention is to express the underlying emotions of a topic and expressing it with the tone you use, the facial expressions you show and the body language you exhibit, to create interest and hold their attention. Frown, smile, show exasperation, the emotion that accurately conveys your position, and strengthens it.

- Where appropriate or when you have built a sufficient level of rapport, touch them physically to get their attention. It's socially acceptable to touch an acquaintance on the forearm or shoulder to get their attention. You can then combine them with the methods above to reinforce the attention they have given you.

- Another popular method is initiating a topic you know the other person is passionate about and segue it gradually and carefully into your topic. Ensure there is a valid/tangible connection between the topics, so the change of the conversation flow doesn't seem abrupt.
- Or simply begin with a planned statement that highlights the benefits your position entails and effectively conveys your position.
- **Need.** Now that you have captured the attention of the person you want to persuade, work on keeping it. A person's focus is a strange thing; it's easier to lose it than getting it in the first place. A question every person asks him or herself when speaking to someone is what is the point of the conversation, why should they continue to listen to you?

You should ask yourself questions like: What do they want? What do they Value? Why would they listen to what you have to say? As you start getting the answers to these questions only then will you be able to hook the person you want to persuade, by speaking about what they care about.

Satisfaction. This step is about providing satisfaction regarding the need you created as described in the previous step. This is the step where you will prove you are a man of your words and build credibility that is valued. The solutions you provide ideally shouldn't create more problems and be a one-time solution to a serious issue or prevent a problematic situation.

Visualization. Visualization is one of the important aspects of every persuasion tactic. It involves drawing a creative yet convincing picture of what you have to offer, how you can improve their situation, or how your decision can benefit them.

The best way to approach this tactic is describing what's in it for them in a detailed and visual manner. For example:

- Picture what it would be like if you never have to do xyz again
- Cut your workload in half by doing xyz (boost your profits, solve your issues)
- Imagine improving your life with xyz, a little change that can work wonders for you

Action. When your persuasion is beginning to have an effect, it will become evident from what the person says, the body language, and the tone of voice, all of which has been discussed in detail in the previous chapters.

As you sense an agreement is approaching, your immediate goal is to lock it in by suggesting a call to action or the next step that'll put your idea or decision in motion. Waiting at this point is futile, best described as a misfire, act ASAP so the only option available to that person is yours. Never let your object of persuasion ponder things over, it usually ends in them changing their minds. Seal the deal.

Integrity Principle

To sum it all up, one assumes the position of a leader when trying to influence or persuade someone. But you won't be a leader unless you are acknowledged as one, and it is only done through exhibiting a trait known as integrity.

Integrity is simply defined as staying true to your words, with your actions backing up your statements. Before you expect people to be persuaded by your words demonstrate yourself to be trustworthy. To put it simply you cannot ask other people to believe your words just because you say so, you have to show it.

Integrity isn't a trait you can turn on and off, it's a lifestyle. It takes a lot of effort to build a reputation, especially honoring everything you say. Most importantly being an example of what you expect from others, even in stressful times, can be a very daunting task. However, developing integrity can be extremely beneficial and increases your persuasive power.

So if you're wondering how one can implement integrity into their lives, there are key areas to focus on developing. They are as follows:

- Sincerity
- Consistency
- Substance

Sincerity. Being authentic, projecting yourself exactly as you are:

- Never put up a false front
- Accepting responsibility for your mistakes
- Striving to meet the commitments made
- Being honest in general, especially about your limitations and what you are capable of delivering

Consistency. Values people can trust and rely on indefinitely, instead of changing face to suit every situation.

- Equally treating your acquaintances
- Keeping your word and fulfilling promises
- Working harder than what is expected of you
- Believing the rules that apply to everyone else apply to you as well, never entertaining double standards.

Substance. This part refers to what has been said earlier, making integrity your lifestyle. Part of your personal and professional versions encompassing all types of relationships.

- Private information stays private. Things said in confidence, are buried with you.
- Avoid complaining and gossiping about a team member with others in the office

- Making decisions that consider what's best for every member of the team, and all those who are likely to be affected by your decision, except competitors of course.
- Giving due credit to those who deserve it
- Investing your time and energy in the development of people who either work for you or depend on you.
- Your priority is to maintain crystal-clear communication while considering and tackling any conflicts that may arise.

After reading the above if you realized you haven't always acted with integrity, you aren't alone. Moreover, keep in mind that integrity is built not with what you say you would do, but rather what you do, one action at a time. Once, you start seeing the results your integrity has reaped, you are guaranteed to keep on going.

Storytelling

Let me list for you the important general highlights of telling a good story. These are given in no particular order because each situation and story deserves individual attention. But here are the important ideas:

- Get your audience involved in the story by using voice dynamics, hand gestures, and facial cues --- the idea is to make your audience visualize they are in the situation of the story --- oh, and a physical story requires clear physical description (be animated, it's funnier).
- Use descriptive terms that appeal to the five senses to draw a better picture for your audience --- sight, sound, smell, taste, feel.
- Attempt to pace the story in accordance with the "pace" of your audience, that is, if your audience is relaxed, then the delivery can afford to be slower. If your audience is hurried, or moving, or has a shorter attention span, speed up the delivery.

- Some stories might be enhanced if told with an accent or in a dialect of some type --- use your judgment with regard to its appropriateness AND with your ability to deliver a convincing voice.
- Feel free to tailor your story to your style and your audience --- you never have to tell it the way it's written or even the same way twice.
- Do not mince words, enunciate clearly --- stay with the story --- keep your audience focused Try to relate to your audience by making eye contact with a few members --- show them you care about them getting it and they'll be more attentive Avoid all the common clichés in delivering your stories --- they are distracting and appear uninventive and unoriginal.
- Use pregnant pauses for dramatic effect --- used sparingly, a good pause makes a funny story even funnier --- it takes some people a second or two longer to get themselves ready for a punchline anyway.
- Normally a casual entrance into a joke or story is best. Begin with "...so I was walking..." or "...I heard about this woman..." or "...there was this guy..." I have found that beginning with "Did you hear about..." or "I have a good joke..." or "Let me tell you a good one I heard..." makes most people kind of uncomfortable because now they feel they have to listen. The more casual approach lets the listeners draw themselves into the story.
- Sometimes a mid-joke reference to something familiar to the listener is helpful. If you are describing, say, a large sandwich, describe it in terms your audience will visualize (a hero, a Dagwood, a Subway, a hoagie, a submarine sandwich) --- that is, always tailor your story to the audience for maximum effect Remember your story (the setup) is as much or more important as the punchline --- after all, you

ARE trying to entertain, aren't you? Don't rush just to get to the punchline --- milk the story for all it's worth.

- The longer stories are harder to learn but are often more impressive to your audience. If it's a complicated story that they couldn't remember well enough to tell themselves, they will be more impressed with your skill --- and more apt to listen to you the next time you have a clever story.
- Naturally gauge your audience's tolerance to profanity, adult topics and adjust your story accordingly. Timely use of profanity can be quite effective for emphasis but be careful not to turn off your audience. The same goes for stories of questionable taste. Always err on the side of being non-offensive. A handy rule of thumb is: "Could I tell this story to the PTA at my children's school?"
- Practice is the key. Anything worth doing, it is worth doing well. Practice with your significant other, buddy or anyone who will put up with your new attempts and humor. Even use a tape recorder. Gauge their feedback (laughter or lack of it) and compensate for it the next time you tell the story.

The main thing is to get started sharing your story. Create a YouTube channel and test your stories on a worldwide platform! After trying a few different types of exposures, you will learn the best way to present your story. When you get enough views on YouTube, you will be ready to make a full studio video. Someone is waiting to hear your ideas, so go let your words be like fire.

REFERENCES

Ader R. Psychoneuroimmunology. New York NY: Academic Press: 1991. American Psychological Association, March 20, 2006, Psychological Science, Research in Action, Multitasking: Switching costs, http://www.apa.org/research/action/multitask. aspx

Ausubel, N., (1948) A Treasure of Jewish Folklore: A Parable That Inspires. F Crown Publishers, New York

Baime, M. J., Meditation and Mindfulness. Essentials of Complementary and Alternative Medicine, ed. Wayne B. Jonas and Jeffrey S. Levin. New York: Lippincott, Williams and Wilkins, 1999.

Bandler, R. and Grinder, J. (1975) The Structure of Magic I. Palo Alto, CA: Science & Behavior Books, Inc.

Bodkin JA, Amsterdam JD, Transdermal selegiline in major depression: a double-blind, placebo-controlled, parallel group study in outpatients. American Journal of Psychiatry 2002; 159: 1869-75.

Bunker, L., Williams, J. M., & Zinsser, N. (1993). Cognitive techniques for improving performance and self-confidence. In J. M. Williams (Ed.), Applied sport psychology: Personal growth to peak performance. Mountain View, CA: Mayfield.

Cousins, N. (1979). Anatomy of an illness. New York, NY: Norton.

Cousins, N. (1989). Head first. The biology of hope. New York NY: Dutton.

Covey, S.R (1990). The Seven Habits of Highly Successful People. New York NY: Free Press

Dillon K, Baker K. Positive emotional states and enhancement of the immune system. International J Psychiatry in Medicine. 1985; 5(1).

Draganski, Gaser, et al. Changes in grey matter induced by training. Nature. 427:311-312 (2004).

Emoto, M. (June 1999). Messages from Water, Vol. 1.

Emmons, R. A., & McCullough, M. E. (2003). Counting blessings versus burdens: An experimental investigation of gratitude and subjective well-being in daily life. Journal of Personality and Social Psychology, 84, 377–89. http://dx.doi.org/10.1037/0022-3514.84.2.377

Festinger, L., (1957). A Theory on Cognitive Dissonance. Stanford University Press, Redwood City, CA

Ginty, D. Johns Hopkins Medicine. (2012, January 11). Touching a nerve: How every hair in skin feels touch and how it all gets to the brain. ScienceDaily. Retrieved March 5, 2018, from www.sciencedaily.com/releases/2012/01/120111103354.htm

Gardner, A. (2010). The power of words. Retrieved from https://www.youtube.com/watch?v=Hzgzim5m7oU

Gopher, D., Armony, L. & Greenspan, Y. (2000). Switching tasks and attention policies. Journal of Experimental Psychology: General, 129, 308-229.

Hardy, L., Jones, G., & Gould, D. (1998). Understanding psychological preparation for sport: Theory and practice of elite performers, West Sussex, UK: John Wiley & Sons.

Heerema, E. MSW, Chaves, C. MD. Can Laughter Yoga Benefit People With Dementia? Updated January 03, 2018.https://www.verywellhealth. com/can-laughter-yoga-benefit-people-with-dementia-98669

Hrobjartsson, A., & Norup, M. (2003). The use of placebo interventions in medical practice, a national questionnaire survey of Danish clinicians. Evaluation & the Health Professions 26, 153–65.

Hughes, M. 2002, Technical Communication, Vol 49, No. 3, pp. 275-285, Society for Technical Communications

Hundley, T. L. (2008) How can I lose with the stuff I use? Columbia, SC: Fit for the King. Journal of Food Science

Korb, A. (2012, November 20). The Grateful Brain. Retrieved August 29, 2017, https://www.psychologytoday.com/blog/prefrontal-nudity/201211/the-grateful-brain

Le Bon, Gustave (1895). The Crowd. A Study of the Popular Mind. Dover publications, Inc., Mineola, NY

Leuchter, A., Cook, I., Witte, E., Morgan, M., Abrams, D., View Author and Article Information Published online: January 01, 2002 Department of Psychiatry and Biobehavioral Sciences, David Geffen School of Medicine at UCLA, University of California Los Angeles, 760 Westwood Plaza, Rm. 57-455, Los Angeles, CA, 90024-1759, USA https://doi.org/10.1176/appi.ajp.159.1.122

Mandal, A. (2017, February) Dopamine Functions. Retrieved March 24, 2018, https://www.news-medical.net/health/dopaminefunctions.aspx

Martin, B. (2018). Challenging Negative Self-Talk. *Psych Central.* Retrieved on May 21, 2018, fromhttps://psychcentral.com/lib/ challenging-negative-self-talk/

Mayo Clinic Staff (2017, February) Retrieved February 25, 2017 https://www.mayoclinic.org/healthy-lifestyle/stress-management/in-depth/positive-thinking/art-20043950?pg=1

Mehrabian, A., and Ferris, S.R. (1967), Inference of Attitudes from Nonverbal Communication in Two Channels, Journal of Consulting Psychology, 31, 3, 48-258

Monroe, A. H. (1943). Monroe's Principles of Speech (military edition). Scott, Foresman and Company. Glenview, IL

Naparstek, B. (1994) Staying Well with Guided Imagery Reed Business Information, Inc, New York, NY

Nierenberg, G. & Calero, H. (1981) The new art of negotiating: How to close any deal. Square One Publishers, Garden City Park, NY

Nierenberg, C. (2009, October 13). Optical illusions: When your brain can't believe your eyes. ABC News. Retrieved from http://abcnews. go.com/Health/EyeHealth/ optical-illusions-eye-brain-agree/ story?id=8455573

O'Donnell, D. (2009). Water documentary - Masaru Emoto's rice experiment. Retrieved from https://youtu.be/Wc-ZmvxfBxE

Oxford (2018) https://en.oxforddictionaries.com/definition/illusion, Oxford University Press

Plous, S. (1993) The Psychology of Judgment and Decision Making. McGraw-Hill, New York, NY

Rattue, G. (2012, January 12). How our sense of touch works. MNT. Retrieved from http://www.medicalnewstoday.com/ articles/240273.php

Rogers, R. & Monsell, S. (1995). The costs of a predictable switch between simple cognitive tasks. Journal of Experimental Psychology: General, 124, 207-231.

Rutz, D., Real Patch Adams says jokes aid practical medicine. January 11, 1999, posted at: 2:28 p.m. EDT. http://www.cnn. com/HEALTH/9901/11/patch.adams/

Schmitz, T. et al (2009). Opposing Influences of Affective State Valence on Visual Cortical Encoding. J. Neuroscience.

Seaward BL. Reframing: Creating a positive mind-set. In: Essentials of Managing Stress. 4th ed. Burlington, Mass.: Jones & Bartlett Learning; 2017.

Selye, H. (1956). The stress of life. New York, NY: McGraw-Hill.

Selye, H. Stress Without Distress. New York NY: Lippincott and Crowell Publishers; 1974.

Severin, Frank T. Humanistic Psychology. The Encyclopedia of Psychiatry, Psychology, and Psychoanalysis. New York: Henry Holt and Co., 1996.

Sinfield, J., Gustafson, T., Hindo, B. The Discipline of Creativity. MIT Sloan Management Review. Published on: Dec 28, 2013https://sloanreview.mit.edu/article/the-discipline-of-creativity/#article-authors

Sood A. The Mayo Clinic Guide to Stress-Free Living. Cambridge, Mass.: Da Capo Press/Lifelong Books; 2013

Stone A, Cox DS, Neale JM, Valdimarsdottir H, and Jandorf L. Evidence that secretory IgA antibody is associated with daily mood. J Personality & Social Psychology. 1987; 52(5):988-993.

Stott, C., (2004) An integrated approach to crowd psychology and public order policing, Policing: An International Journal of Police Strategies & Management, Vol. 27 Issue: 4, pp.558-572. Emerald Group Publishing Limited, Bingley BD, WA, United Kingdom

Tame, A. C., Amazing Activities for Low Function Abilities and Caregiver Guide. Once an adult Twice a Child. iUniverse LLC., Bloomington, IN 2017

Tentmaker Ministries. (n.d.). Fire in the Bible. Retrieved from http://www.tentmaker.org/BreakingBread/1.html

Treese, A. 2009. http://www.sciencedirect.com/science/article/pii/S027826260900236X. Retrieved July 14, 2016.

Waitley, D., The Psychology of Winning: Ten Qualities of a Total Winner, Berkley, New York NY, 1984

Wedmore, J. (date) stated, in an ad for Entrepreneurs Content Marketing Strategy, Zhan et al., 2009

Whitbourne, S.K., (2013). Make Your Self-Talk Work for You: Learn from the pros how to use constructive, not dysfunctional, and self-talk. https://www.psychologytoday.com/us/blog/fulfillmentany-age/201309/make-your-self-talk-work-you. Posted Sep 10, 2013

Willis, J. and Todorov, A., First Impressions, Psychological Science vol. 17 issue 7, pages 592-598, July 1, 2006

Willis M. T., Placebo Alters Brain Function January 2, 2015 http://abcnews.go.com/Health/Depression/story?id=117057&page=1

Wooten P. Laughter as therapy for patient and caregiver. In Hodgkin J, Connors G, Bell C, eds. Pulmonary Rehabilitation. Philadelphia PA: Lippincott; 1993.

ABOUT THE AUTHOR

Indianapolis, Indiana was a great place to grow up in the 70's. The west side was the up and coming area; although the east side had pockets of suburban neighborhoods, it still had acres of undeveloped land. When I was very young my parents separated. My mother worked as a nurse's aide at a local hospital while going to school to become a registered nurse. Each morning would get my older brothers and me ready for school. She would see them off, then drop me off at the daycare on her way to work.

At night she would study by reading to me. Sometimes the reading wasn't a story at all. The so-called stories were actually her nursing reading assignments. Well, I guess she had to kill two birds with one stone. My mother didn't really do a lot of baby talk stuff. She spoke to us very plainly. I imagine that's how I learned to talk so early.

One day my mother sent some breakfast with me when she dropped me off at the daycare. The daycare worker didn't want to give me the food that was sent with me. She gave me the same food as what she gave the other kids. But I knew my mother wanted me to eat what she sent with me. I didn't eat the food the worker gave me. When the day was over my mother came to pick me up. It just so happened that my grandmother came to the house shortly after my mother and I got home. While my mother went to start dinner, my grandmother and I sat in the living room. Grandma asked me, "How was your day at school"? My explanation about not eating was unacceptable for my grandmother. My grandmother was very loving, but also an extremely protective woman. Especially of me. By the time my mother came out of the kitchen, grandma had already packed my bags. She told my mother, "He's coming to stay with me." So from the time I was 2 years old until I was sixteen, I lived with my grandmother. As I got older I split my summer vacation between my mother's house and my grandmother's house.

During my childhood, I wasn't one of the best academic students. Although my grandparents were extremely wise, they did not have a lot of education, nor did they put a lot of emphasis on it. As long as I had passing grades they were fine with it. In fact, I would sit in class and draw pictures, write poems, etc. I would even write plans on how I could make money. Although I was beaming with creativity and knowledge, I lacked the necessary focus for my school work. My teachers seemed to lack the ability to recognize my potential or at best they didn't know how to extract the good from within.

My family had to endure several years of my struggling just barely make a passing grade. A couple of times it was suggested that I be placed in a class with students who had learning disabilities, but my mother said, "No, he just needs to try harder." It was only through the grace of God, that I made it to the 8th grade. So here I was, an 8th grader with a 4th-grade reading comprehension level. I was moved through the system without the correct skill set for an 8th grader.

In my mind, my peers seemed to grasp everything. When scholastics came up, I felt like I was alone even though I may have been surrounded by family and friends. The problem was I was afraid to ask for help and by the time I did, I was so far behind I would get too frustrated to catch up.

I lived with my grandparents during the school year, but as I got older most of my summers were spent at my mother's house on the other side of town. My two older brothers lived with my mom all year long. Kevin was the middle son. I guess he had that middle child syndrome pretty bad because he was extremely smart but equally annoying. Kevin would pick on me all the time.

One of the things he loved was to try to impress our friends with was his knowledge of African American history. He also seemed to enjoy using it to show my ignorance of history. He would talk about the writings of W.E.B. DuBois, the patents of George Washington Carver, the blood bank created by Charles Richard Drew, and he even said that George Crum created the potato chip. I thought, "Now that's going too far! He's got to be lying." He even had the audacity to tell me Africans discovered the Americas 170 years before Christopher Columbus. I thought, here's my chance to prove him wrong. I'm going to the library and get the real facts and show everyone he's wrong...I rode my bike to the library and started to dig for information. "I've got him now!" I said....What! To my surprise, he was right. An African monarch abdicated his throne in 1311 and set off to discover if the large body of water, that we now know as the Atlantic Ocean, like the vast River Niger, "had another river bank." It was hard to believe, but he was correct. Right about it all. If this was true then what else could be locked away inside of some book. What about other possibilities?

I began to read the various encounters of ordinary people, (just like me) doing extraordinary things. This sent my mind racing. I started reading more books and articles; in fact, I read so much each day that my reading comprehension began to rise. Kevin unknowingly changed my motivation paradigm. From that day forward, the desire to learn more and be more has never left. My big brother Kevin unknowingly sparked a flame of passion for knowledge in me. Even greater than the passion for knowledge, that spark illuminated a path to all kinds of possibilities.

"To learn how to think is to learn how to live" – Ernest Holmes

The new-found desire to learn helped me to become a better student; not just scholastically, but a more observant student of life itself. Sophocles stated, "Always desire to learn something useful." (Oedipus Rex, 429 BC) I believe understanding and using simple methods of communicating directed to reach a specific audience is one of the most useful things anyone can learn. Floyd Maxwell once wrote: "Perhaps the greatest joy is learning how to motivate yourself" (Floyd Maxwell, 1957), published in Q9 magazine on August 21, 2001. I knew I had found treasure in books, but I didn't quite know what to do with this newly found interest.

Although my reading comprehension had improved, I still felt as though I was not as bright as the other kids. In many ways, I had taken on a mindset of inferiority in reference to peers from my past. They knew me as the unlearned weak kid. For years I saw myself as an underachiever, so that's exactly what I produced. My anxiety came from viewing myself as the slow, but all of a sudden made grades and conversation started giving me assurance that I was smart.

Even though I had made strides in my confidence, in grade school I always seemed to manage to get out of most presentations in front of the class. The Sunday school teacher at my church assigned a few scriptures for me to say during an Easter program. There was no way to finagle my way out of the program. So I began to search for answers the only way I knew how: I read and prayed.

As I studied and prayed, I began to understand that the words we speak, receive, and believe shape the world around us by changing our thoughts, which in turn direct our actions. The words of the generations before us laid the foundation for what we see in society today.

Some words are spoken, empowered to be carried out. They have been creative and full of enhancements for our lives. Those kinds of words are what we should give to others and seek out for ourselves. Some words taught despair and hopelessness; which have held millions in poverty. When people believe that there is no hope, they settle into a reality defined in not searching for or even recognizing a way out of that situation. But when a hope-filled person hears, reads or takes notice of words and actions of positive faith, there is an opportunity for change.

Once I had finally begun to understand that my fears were because of the words I allowed to get into my mind and the words I let come out of my mouth, I knew that I could begin to change the course of my life. Daily, I reminded myself of what Proverbs 18:21 (KJV) says: "Death and life are in the power of the tongue, and they that love it shall eat the fruit thereof." Modern scholars teach it in a simplified format: The words that you speak can bring you good things that fill your life or things that will destroy your life. This brought to my mind a huge question. If people have the ability to change their lives by saying the right things, then why don't people listen to and speak the good things that they want? How can I find the right words to help myself and my family to have a better life? (Hint)

There was a very simple concept I read in an editorial about a phenomenal speaker. The question is posed in Luke 24:32 "Were not his words burning in our hearts..." I don't recall the speaker who expounded on that quote, but those words match what I had learned years ago. Scriptures, psychology and physiology began to all flow together with my faith. Some philosophers, behavioral psychologists, religious leaders and other truth-seekers give a threefold view of man - A "human being" is a spiritual being that uses a mind and has a body. My favorite teaching of the principle states, "a man is a spirit that has a soul and lives in a body. The soul is your mind, will and emotions" (Pastor G.E. Studdard). Learning to focus my mind on specific thoughts, decide the direction of my will and control the actions behind my emotions has helped me to start the journey of having success in my life.

From studying the victories of other people and patterns of overcoming inner obstacles, I gained control over my fears. Conquering one's fears is the first major step in gaining control over one's life. Even though I had started taking that first step, it was years later when it all came together and clicked for me. Over the years, this simple, but powerful prayer inspired me to help others understand how to make their words powerful and effective...Like

Fire. My prayer became, "Lord, let my words be like fire and the people's heart like wood so that my every word would kindle a flame of fire on the inside of them."

This book is geared toward making your natural words like fire to better communicate and deliver ANY type of message.

Printed in the United States
By Bookmasters